OUR SCHOOL
IN
HAWTHORN ROAD

𝕿𝖍𝖊 𝕶𝖊𝖙𝖙𝖊𝖗𝖎𝖓𝖌 𝕷𝖊𝖆𝖉𝖊𝖗 𝖆𝖓𝖉 𝕺𝖇𝖘𝖊𝖗𝖛𝖊𝖗
FRIDAY, DECEMBER, 28TH, 1894

OUR ANNUAL RETROSPECT
KETTERING DURING 1894

At the April meeting the Board accepted Mr. G.V. Henson's tender of £1,630 for the erection of an infant school in the Hawthorn-road, which building it is expected will be occupied early next year.

i

Written and Compiled by
CARL HOWARD with friends

OUR SCHOOL
IN
HAWTHORN ROAD

"A Sort of a History"

D.L. Photography

STRAGGLER PUBLISHERS

ISBN 978-0-9550911-2-4

Copyright © Carl Howard 2008

Published by:
Straggler Publishers
102 The Pygthle
Wellingborough
Northants
NN8 4RS
01933 678236

Printed by:
Stanley L Hunt (Printers) Ltd
Midland Road
Rushden
Northants
NN10 9UA
01933 356226

-- oOo --

The front cover photograph shows the School outing to The Hilly Hollies, Weldon 1912.

CONTENTS

ACKNOWLEDGEMENTS

PRODUCING this book has given me great satisfaction and grateful thanks are extended to all who helped me, in however small a way. It would be most remiss of me not to first thank the four people without whose joint help and guidance this book could not have been brought to life: Richard Hall, Hawthorn Community School Head Teacher whose help and patience were invaluable, his allowing me the freedom to speak with school staff where necessary and for allowing me access to various school records. Dr. Roy Hargrave for allowing me full access to his Ph.D. thesis entitled "The Life and Works of John Alfred Gotch" which provided me with the foundation for my first chapter. Dereck Lewis of D.L. Photography for his professional expertise and advice with the photographic work and Angela Hill of AMH Typing for her word processing skills, helpful suggestions and ideas.

I must also express gratitude to the following: Hawthorn School staff, who have always been most helpful and informative; Crispin Powell and staff at the Northamptonshire Records Office, together with Northamptonshire County Council for allowing the School plans to be photographed and for allowing access to Kettering Urban District Council School Management and General Purposes Sub-committee minutes 1903-1944; Kettering Borough Council for allowing me to use information gleaned from these minutes: GSS Architecture for approving reproduction of the Hawthorn Road School original drawings; Bernard Hales for kind and valued photographic assistance; Andrea Pettingdale and staff at the Kettering Public Library for assistance with my research; Caroline Morgan and Jeremy Clifford of the Kettering Evening Telegraph for allowing me to use photographs and news from the archives and for their help and understanding; Dr. David Walker for historical information relative to Pollard Evangelical Church; Phil Manning for the use of information from various copies of Kelly's Directories; the English Chess Federation for kind assistance; Tony Sparrow of the Childrens Society for information about St. Gabriels Home; Debbie Whitmore of Wellingborough School for information about Peter Hudson; Dan Hedley, Syndication Executive of the Independent Newspaper for details from the obituary of Lt. General Sir Peter Hudson, M.B.E., C.B.E., K.C.B.; Joan Bambridge for material about her son Christopher; Angela Scheidegger of Northamptonshire County Council for information relating to School Governors; Graham Jones for the loan of the School Centenary Pack; Express and Star Newspaper Stafford for permission to use the Stafford Rangers F.C. photograph; Leicester Photo Services and John Wright Photographers for use of certain school photographs and Helen Jones for allowing me to reproduce her late husband Ian's drawing of the School.

I also wish to acknowledge that Tony Ireson's series of books, "Old Kettering – A view from the 1930's", was a foremost source of valuable background information.

The following were most generous in allowing me to reproduce illustrations from their own collections: Richard Wardle, Isobel Sleigh, Barbara Law, Eddie Giacobbe, Len Foster, Susan Eden, Nick Andic and his siblings, David Needle, John Watson, Bill Bellamy, Mary and Trevor Ashby, Mike Coleman, Maureen Eaton, Maureen Buckerfield, Sue and Jacc Batch, Sonnie Torlot, Adam Cave and Nora Cheatle.

I must also express gratitude to the following for help and advice in so many differing ways: Jill and Ray Toseland, Norma and John Hill, David Short, Vanda Robinson, John Sellars, Bob Carr, Jim Hales, David Ingyon, Janet Deer, Brenda Walker, Eva and Arthur Heath, Ian Addis, Bob Mercer, Sue Wills, Dorothy Webb, Joan Carvell, Ron Greenall, Jane Watson, Alison Bagley, Martin Moloney, Linda Dix, Margaret Watson, Elvin Royall and of course to my wife Eileen for her support and for regular supplies of tea, red wine and more red wine whilst I was working on the book. Thanks to everyone else who contributed with stories and mementoes. I am so grateful to you all.

-- oOo --

DEDICATION

To my late dear Mother, God Bless Her
She would have loved this book, as she loved Hawthorn Road
School

-- oOo --

INTRODUCTION

FROM the beginnings of Hawthorn Road Infants School in 1894, (as the third of Kettering's Board Schools to be build when education was first offered to the masses) through the year 1905 when the large extension was constructed, right up to modern times, this school has been renowned as a happy and friendly place for thousands of children from south western Kettering. Possibly 5000 children have passed through the entrances since 1894, with up to four generations of some families being educated at Hawthorn. The records, memories and photographs within this book have been collected together to provide an insight into the social history of the school and to include changes that have occurred over the past 112 years, not only in school life but in the world outside of that too. The reader will note that this book does not pretend to be a comprehensive school history. It cannot be that as so many school records are missing. However I have utilised material from many written sources but sadly for a considerable period no significant information was found. However in approaching my subject from differing angles through the thirteen chapters, I believe that a most interesting overall picture of the school emerges. I trust that you the reader, will feel likewise.

Carl Howard
Wellingborough, November 2007

-- o0o --   -- o0o --   -- o0o --

KETTERING SCHOOL BOARD

Regulations for the Management of Schools

<u>Moral Instruction Item 11</u>: Moral instruction shall be definitely provided for in the timetable of each school.

Two moral lessons a week of half-an-hour each shall be given to all the children in the mixed schools, and an entry of these lessons shall be made on the timetable. In the Infant's School the number and length of the lessons may be arranged by the Headmistress. The series should include such subjects as obedience to parents, honesty, truthfulness, industry, temperance, courage, kindness, perseverance, frugality and thrift, government of temper, courtesy, unselfishness and kindred moral duties.

The lessons should be of a conversational character and should be largely enforced by illustrations drawn from daily life.

By order of Fredk Wm. Bull – Clerk to the Board
School Board Offices, High Street, Kettering
December 1890

(from the Kettering School Board minute book 29 May 1890 – 22 February 1892)

-- o0o --   -- o0o --   -- o0o --

How times change!!!

Carl Howard – June 2007

ix

Chapter One

In the beginning ......

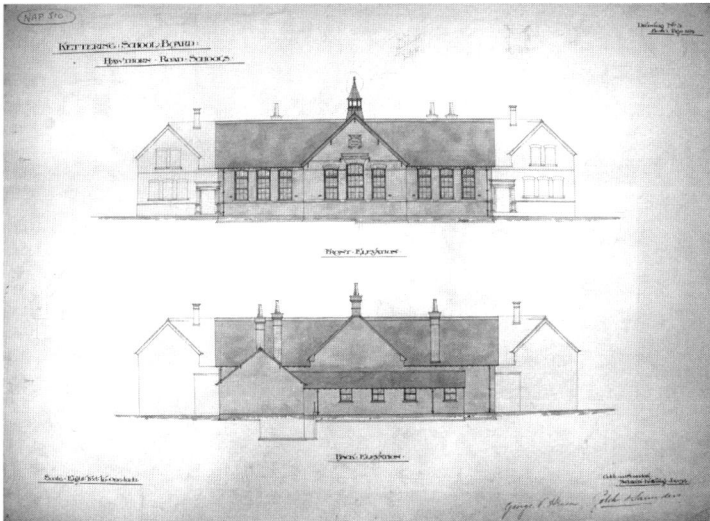

Gotch's Original Drawing 1894

1

IT was the thirty third year of the reign of Queen Victoria, William Gladstone was the Prime Minister, with William Forster (appointed by Gladstone in 1868) as Vice President of the Committee of Council on Education. It was the year that Marie Lloyd and Jan Smuts were born, the year that Charles Dickens and Robert E. Lee passed away, the year that saw Mark Twain married in New York and indeed the year that saw the formation of Derbyshire County Cricket Club. It was the year 1870.

Forster's responsibility was to carry the Education Act through the House of Commons, which he achieved on 17 February 1870. As a result of this Act, School Boards were given power to examine the provision of elementary education within their district, provided then by voluntary societies. Should their conclusion be that there were insufficient places, they could build and maintain schools out of the rates. Eventually Kettering elected a School Board during 1890 with Davis Frederic Gotch as Chairman. His Committee oversaw the building of five schools in Kettering up to 1902, when the School Board became the Local Education Committee.

Stamford Road School (1892) was the first to be built, followed by Rockingham Road (1893), Hawthorn Road (1894-1895), Park Road (1898-1899) and Spencer Street School (1902), later known as The Central School.

At the April 1894 meeting of the Kettering School Board, the Kettering Leader and Observer within its "Our Annual Retrospect Column" told that the School Board had accepted a tender from G.V. Henson (1842-1907) to erect an Infant School in the Hawthorn Road for £1630 (this tender was the lowest submitted). John Alfred Gotch, a former Kettering Grammar School boy, (1852-1942) was the chosen architect.

It may be of interest here to reveal a little of *John Alfred Gotch* and his three brothers, as in many ways they had a profound effect then, on both the people of Kettering and the town itself. Their names and works live on, as for example there are many buildings standing today in the town that were designed by Gotch, who worked from a small office in Gold Street. Charles Saunders joined him in 1887 and together they designed many buildings, including the Midland Bank Head Office in Poultry, London. Locally in Kettering, their buildings included the Art Gallery, St. Mary's Church, the Gold Street Old Post Office block, the schools in

2

Stamford Road, Hawthorn Road, Park Road and Spencer Street, the Midland Bank, part of the General Hospital, the Newland Street/Montague Street corner, Sunnylands (William Timpson's house in Headlands which later became St. Peter's School) and the former Sun Inn in Market Street. Is it unexpected therefore that Kettering at one time was known as "the town that Gotch built"?

Of course the company that he founded with Saunders became in 1930 Gotch, Saunders and Surridge, when Henry Surridge, who joined Gotch and Saunders during 1899 as a junior, became a partner. Today, after well over one hundred years, the business is one of the oldest and most respected within the region, boasting some 60 employees, including partners (February 27th 2007). Gotch became a most authoritative architectural author, having many books to his credit. Indeed, in 1923 his renown was acknowledged when he was elected President of The Royal Institute of British Architects.

During 1938 when Kettering became a Borough, he was appointed Charter Mayor. A marvellous day of celebration was planned for the occasion, including a concert and a civic lunch at which he would receive the Charter from the Lord Lieutenant, the Marquis of Exeter. Sadly the celebrations were cancelled as outside influences took a hand. The country was on the brink of war when Charter Day fell in the midst of the Munich crisis. The Charter was presented therefore in the Regal Cinema (currently Granada Bingo) at a comparatively low key event.

Adam Cave collection

Left to right: Davis Frederic Gotch (the first and only Kettering School Board Chairman), Thomas Cooper Gotch (who painted most of the pictures on the walls behind the group), John Alfred Gotch (architect of Hawthorn Road School) and Henry Gale Gotch (who gave his name to Henry Gotch School), seen in the Alfred East Art Gallery, Kettering, c.1920

3

John Alfred Gotch died in 1942 and was buried at Weekley.

Henry Gale Gotch (1848-1939), the eldest brother, spent over twenty years in the family shoemaking business. He was a director of Mobbs and Lewis, the first Chairman of the Education Committee 1903-1906, twenty years a magistrate, a leading local Liberal politician and Chairman of the Urban Council 1906-1907. He gave his name to The Henry Gotch School.

Davis Frederic Gotch (1850-1935) two years younger than Henry Gale, worked in the family shoe business for many years and became a partner of William Timpson for eight years. He was the first and only Local School Board Chairman between 1890 and 1902.

Thomas Cooper Gotch (1854-1931) was the youngest brother. He spent just three years with the family footwear firm. He then studied art in several parts of the world, including Antwerp and Paris. His pictures attracted much attention and often graced the principal galleries of the world. He ranked both with the great Victorian painters and also amongst the later modern artists.

At this point, the keen eyed reader may have realised that although Forster's Education Act was passed in 1870, Gotch's first school for the Kettering School Board in Stamford Road was not built until over twenty years later. The reason being that public opinion was unfavourable, as during 1871, a poll was taken in Kettering to consider the wisdom of creating a Kettering School Board. The vote was lost. A further poll was taken in 1877 and the vote was lost by an even larger margin than that of six years previously. The good people of Kettering obviously didn't care for a rate increase, not even to educate their children!

However, as Kettering's population was growing quite quickly, it was eventually realised that there were insufficient elementary school places within the Parish. A final notice was therefore issued by the Education Department from Whitehall during January 1890, *demanding* the supply of education for 900 children. The first Kettering School Board was thus elected some four months later, with Davis Frederic Gotch as Chairman.

Following the building of Stamford Road School by Gotch (who took twenty-two months to deliver his building) and the building of Rockingham Road School by H.A. Cooper (who took thirty-seven

4

months), Gotch became the sole architect for the Kettering School Board.

During May 1893 the Board appointed a Committee to investigate the need for a school at the southern end of Kettering. The Committee decided to recommend a school which would provide for 200 infants. The Education Department duly sanctioned the Committee's recommendation in September of that year and a plot, virtually in the centre of Hawthorn Road, of 2776 square yards was purchased for £880 from Charles Pollard.

Charles Pollard was a very well known local figure and indeed was recognized as the best popular public speaker in the county. He was an auctioneer, he owned houses in Broadway, where he lived at Cromwell House (which stood where the Hawthorn Community Primary School playground now stands). He also owned houses in Charles Street and Pollard Street; hence the streets were given his name. He was also a nonconformist, a liberal and a champion of the unfortunates as the Kettering Leader and Observer of 7 October 1892 tells us: "No man has keener or truer sympathy with the oppressed and the helpless, and his aggressive fervour against alcohol and vaccination is due to much worthier reasons than a mere love of prominence. He has convinced himself that his action is for the public good and he pursues his way with a tenacity which has had considerable success."

Hawthorn Road School Statement of Cost			
	£	S	D
Purchase of site (from Charles Pollard)	880	0	0
Legal and other expenses	23	9	3
Builder (G V Henson)	1630	0	0
Architect (J Alfred Gotch)	92	10	6
Clerk of Works	40	15	0
Heating & Ventilation	50	0	0
Furniture	81	12	10
Gas Co	1	15	6
£2800	**3**	**1**	

5

In 1891 Charles Pollard had the London Road Hall built (also known as the London Road Mission Hall) at the corner of Broadway and London Road, as he found the routine of the Baptist denomination too conventional for his tastes. Yet it wasn't until 1946 that the Chapel became known as Pollard Memorial Church, during the time that Reverend Andrew Sinden was it's minister. Then later during the early 1990's it gradually became known as Pollard Evangelical Church.

I remember my mother telling me that my grandfather, Ralph Musgrave (express train driver, London Midland and Scottish line and local lay preacher) used to preach from the pulpit of London Road Hall during the 1920s. Mother used to accompany him in her singing capacity. She had quite a good voice and usually sang two solos. She used to very much enjoy these occasions as both she and my grandfather used to have tea with the Pollard family at Cromwell House prior to the service.

However, the chosen site for the school to the rear of Cromwell House was larger than initially required. The architects took a possible extension into their plans, for there was no method then of estimating a rise in the population. So a school was designed to house 226 infants with an option of having a further 330 at a later date.

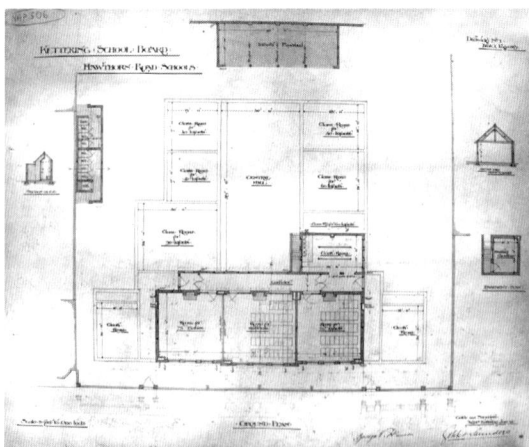

D.L. Photography

Architects plan of the School 1894

6

The builders moved onto the site in 1894 – George Valentine Henson (1842-1907) was a local man who had his yard in Eskdaill Street. He was an experienced builder having many houses and the Kettering Cattle Market Buildings to his credit, along with the restoration of both Cransley and Hargrave Churches. He was a man of many talents who lived in Sondes House on the corner of Broadway and Headlands. His was the end house of a block of seven. The next door neighbour was David Brown, who was postmaster at the Gold Street GPO. The kindly David invited the Hensons: George, wife and daughters, around to his home just prior to Christmas 1907 for a social evening of piano and song. George had a good voice and proved his worth with four songs during the course of the evening. He was ready to return home when he suddenly collapsed into a chair and died. He was 65.

The 1903 edition of Kelly's Directories tells us that "Hawthorn Road Infants School (erected 1894-1895) opened during May 1895 (May 1) with _220_ infants, the average attendance being 116. Miss Elizabeth Anne Clarke – Mistress."

Under the legislation of the day the School was financed from three distinct sources:

1.   by a Government grant, based on the attendance record, together with test results of the pupils;
2.   by the local rate; and
3.   by parental fees (maximum 9 pence per week). During 1891 however the Government responded to growing pressure from the Trade Union Congress amongst others, regarding these fees, with an Act which required all school districts to provide free places (within 12 months) for the children of all parents requiring these. By the end of the century no parent was paying these fees without wishing to do so. The residue of elementary school fees however was not finally abolished until 1918.

Kettering Population
1881 – 11,095   1891 – 19,454   1901 – 28,653   1905 – 30,000

The possible extensions to the school that Gotch had planned were soon to become a reality. However, they did have to be modified as when we see the expanding population figures, we perhaps understand why.

7

Two wings were to be added to provide cloakrooms and the entrances would be adjacent to the appropriate playgrounds – entrance for boys and infants to the side and that for girls to the rear. The interior would also be redesigned and extended to accommodate six classrooms, emptying into a central hall. Each classroom would have between 32 and 60 children. A total of 268 children would be initially housed within the extension. Above the classrooms and cloakrooms were to be two mistresses rooms, a master's room, a cookery classroom, bookstore and staff toilets.

O.P. Drever, a well established local builder who had a yard in St. Michael's Road, won the contract to build the extension, which he delivered in precisely six months. The contract price for the new building was £3717.17s.0d.

Whilst the revised plans were being drawn up, the Kettering School Board had been disbanded and so the commissioning clients were the Kettering Education Committee, who took over from the School Board in 1902.

The extension was completed during late 1905 and officially opened on Tuesday 31 October, which early morning promised a typical grey autumn day, as the string of carriages bringing the dignitaries of Kettering began to arrive in Hawthorn Road for the formal opening of the newly enlarged Hawthorn Road Council School.

It was an impressive group that appeared to mark the opening ceremony: Mr. H.G. Gotch (Chairman of the Kettering Educational Committee) who presided, supported by Mr. J. Bond (Clerk), Mr. C. Saunders (Gotch Saunders), Mr. R.B. Wallis (Chairman of the Finance Sub-Committee) and Mr. L. Holland (Secretary of the County Educational Committee).

Others present included the Rector of Kettering, Messrs A. Mackay, A.G. Jones, F. Toseland, A. Lewis, A.H. Bryan, C.L. Wilson, Mrs. C.W. Lane, Mrs. D.F. Gotch (members of the Education Committee).

Messrs E. Bradley, C. Henson (members of Kettering Urban Council), S. York, (School Attendance Officer), D.F. Gotch, A. Webb, R.C. Wrigley, Rev. Father Tonks.

8

Messrs J.H. Wallis (Grammar School Governor), J.G. Anderson, J.J. Rawson, H.J.H. Bye, R.H. Vickers, C.W. Lane, O.S. Rainstrick, J.H. Gill and Mr. W.H. Cartwright (newly appointed Headmaster of the School).

There was also a large number of ladies, including headmistresses of various schools. (In the Church Walk Infants School log of November 1905 the Headmistress, Miss Mary Theophenia Shayler records: "By invitation of the Educational Council attended the opening of the new school in Hawthorn Road".)

In his address, the Chairman said that, at the origination of the Schools' Board in 1892, the town's population was 20,000 with average school attendance of 3,300. At the present time (1905) the population had risen to 30,000 with average attendance of 5,500.

The Chairman believed that the Authority was "doing the right thing in opening a small school with classrooms for not an unreasonable amount of scholars. The speciality of the new school", he said, "was in regard to the structure which was known as Fireproof."

In the selection of a headmaster for the school, the Chairman explained that the committee had chosen Mr. W.H. Cartwright, a gentleman who had done good work for many years as an assistant master and later, as a first assistant at Port Sunlight.

Mr. Cartwright's assistant would be very important, he said, and he mentioned Miss Cox who had "done long work in Kettering".

Mr. Gotch stressed that the school should have plenty of books to encourage the children to educate themselves.

He went on to add "an important proviso" – that the child should be developing not only his brain, but his hands and his handiwork.

As Mr. Gotch announced the formal opening of the Hawthorn Road Council School, the autumn sun broke through the October clouds – a sign that augured a bright future for the new school.

The Headmaster, Mr. W.H. Cartwright said that "he would do his utmost to make the school a thorough success" (applause).

9

Mr. R.B. Wallis proposed a vote of thanks to the architects.

For the architects, Mr. C. Saunders replied and thanked Mr. Wallis and the builder, Mr. O.P. Drever, "who had carried out the building of the school in such a short time".

The Rector of Kettering proposed a vote of thanks to Mr. Gotch (the Chairman) and said it was a great pleasure to think that all those present at the opening were united in one great purpose of education – whether they were 'Patriots', 'Imperialists' or 'Citizens' of the wider empire, they had one object in common – in doing the best they could for the boys and girls. They were working together towards one great end.

Mr. A. Webb seconded and the Chairman, in reply, spoke of the valuable help of Mr. Bond (Clerk) who had given a great deal of thought, care and attention to the new building, from its beginning to this, the opening day.

The meeting then dispersed and many availed themselves of the opportunity of inspecting the new school ... (Thus reported The Kettering Guardian of 3 November 1905).

-- oOo --   -- oOo --   -- oOo --

Chapter Two

Subsequent Extensions, Additions and Enhancements

Opening of Swimming Pool – 1964

POSSIBLY to be expected the School has not always been exactly the right size for its catchment area. For example during the mid 1960s and into the early 1970s the mobile classrooms almost flowed into the school grounds, as the building was full to bursting. In fact, during 1972 the School roll extended to 542 pupils for the summer term! Yet, when we look at September 1980 the last mobile was removed as the roll showed a total of 263 pupils.

Most interested parties were quite relieved when the old HORSA (Hutted Operation for Raising the School Age) building was demolished during 1990 and removed from the site. It had done its duty for almost 50 years. The school canteen, along with two classrooms, had been housed within for some time, but the building was now quite scruffy and badly in need of repair and refurbishment. It was felt therefore that it had served its purpose and the chosen option was complete removal! In its place as confirmed by the local council authority during September 1990, a mobile dining room and two classrooms would be sited within school grounds.

However, rather strong objections were received from a Garfield Street resident to this plan, as it was claimed that his property would be overlooked by any such classrooms. Following discussion between the interested parties, the matter was resolved by the School agreeing to plant a tree to screen the end of his garden.

During Summer 1991 the old brick play barn was part demolished to allow the McAlpine site huts to be installed. These had been acquired at no charge, due to a downturn in the building trade and were at that time surplus to McAlpine's requirements. These buildings when refurbished accommodated the newly created Playschool and on this occasion planning permission had gone through quite quickly. The School itself had funded this exercise.

During 1993, the Head and Governors decided that an extension to include a community room, a library and toilets was desirable. The plan was therefore to channel profit made over the Centenary celebrations due to commence later in 1993, into a Hawthorn Centenary Building Fund. At this very early stage an amount of £100,000 was considered to be an appropriate sum to completely pay for the extension. Plans for suitable Centenary functions began to be put into place therefore, in order to raise funds for this most ambitious project. Money didn't come along too easily however and not until October 1996 could a planning application be submitted to Kettering Borough Council. Approval was granted during late December of that year. Tenders were called for and the quotations varied between £93,000 and £126,000. Messrs Warren & Warren Building Services of Meadow Road, Kettering won the contract.

£40,000 was obtained from Northants County Council for promoting community affairs, £10,000 was granted from the local Borough Council and, as reported within the columns of the Kettering Evening Telegraph of 15th October 1997, a magnificent sum of £65,000 was raised by the School, pupils and teachers, together with the PTA, to total £115,000 towards enhancing the School building.

The project was finally completed on 14th November 1997. Phil Sawford, the local Labour MP had officially opened the extension on 9th October 1997 some 5 weeks prior!

A further planning application was submitted during March 1998 for a three-classroom extension and covered play area directly to the rear of the school. This was granted some two months later and the extension was duly completed and informally opened, again by Phil Sawford, MP on Friday 25th June 1999.

The PTA had contributed £4,500 towards the cost of £235,000. The balance being known as "New deal for schools money," was paid by the government, administered by the Local Authority. In addition, a further loan of £12,000 had been agreed with the County Council for toilet refurbishment at this time, thus the total expenditure on enhancing the school amounted to £247,000.

Following much thought and research by Head Teacher Richard Hall, permission was further requested during mid-2002 for the erection of a new timber-framed changing room block, which would double as an IT section during autumn and winter. The swimming pool changing rooms were now beyond repair. The cost of a new substantial wooden structure would be around £35,000. A comparative brick building would cost nearly £85,000, so four firms were contacted, with costs expected to be in the following areas:

13

The ICT. Suite/Swimming pool changing room,
within the oak framed wooden building 2003

The building	£35,000	-	£40,000
Groundwork and demolition	£12,000	-	£13,000
Electrics and professional fees	£4,000	-	£5,000
Total being between	**£51,000**	and	**£58,000**

The school was given the go-ahead. Heritage Buildings were chosen and the work when completed was considered to be of an excellent, high quality nature and a great asset to the school.

-- oOo --

During mid 1963 the local Evening Telegraph reported that it was the intention of Hawthorn County Primary School to raise £500 by April 1964 in order to fund a swimming pool to be built within the school grounds. The intention was to site the pool between the HORSA block canteen and the school buildings in the Junior Girls playground. The money would be raised by school functions, in a joint venture between the teaching staff and the PTA. The fund-raising moved along to plan, so that during February 1964 work began on the project, under the stewardship of teacher David Arden, with Bob Scotney, a most capable lieutenant. Weekend working parties carried out all the work on the pool, which was

14

designed to offer teaching facilities to non-swimmers and beginners.

Swimming pool construction 1964 – early days

The timetable was successfully adhered to, as the official opening, on 29th April 1964 was made by Alderman Walter Dyson, himself a School Manager, and a keen swimmer in his youth. Headmaster D.A. Woods spoke of the great contribution made by staff and parents to the project, especially the groundwork. He was followed by Councillor C.W. Godfrey, Chairman of the School Managers and Kettering Mayor elect, who further congratulated the PTA on a fine achievement. A presentation was then made to Mr. Arden in appreciation of his efforts.

Originally the pool was not heated but during the early 1980's a new modern heating and filtration system was fitted, which it was hoped, would enable the children to use the pool more regularly in the future.

Hawthorn County Primary School was the first Primary School in Kettering to enjoy a do-it-yourself swimming pool. Several other schools in the area followed suit over later years, thus encouraging more local youngsters to swim.

Eddie Giacobbe (1959-1965) has the last word on this topic:

"The kids had to shuffle through a tray of disinfectant before getting in," he told me, *"and I used polystyrene floats whilst learning to swim."*

-- oOo --   -- oOo --   -- oOo --

15

Chapter Three

My Story

Northamptonshire County Council Education Commit....

HAWTHORN ROAD SCHOOL KETTERING

Report on ..Carl...Howard......   Age..10.7m.......

Position in Age Group..../l....out of..62. children.

Position in Form ..../l.....out of..41. children.

English......Fair............   Geography...Good.............

Reading......Fair............   History...Fair................

Arithmetic....Fair............   Nature.....Good..............

Handwork.....Satisfactory.....   Art.......Satisfactory.........

Writing & Spelling V.fair. S. Satisfactory   Physical Training..Good.......

Attendance.....Regular.......   Behaviour..Satisfactory........

REMARKS Carl could do better.

Form Teacher.M.Gudging.date 24/12/47.....Headmaster.....

I won't comment! (C.H. February 2008)

IT was a fine morning during late August 1941 and I had never given school much thought until that time. However, it was 8.40 a.m. and having been washed and dressed rather earlier than usual, I found myself being taken by Mother across the Broadway into Argyle Street, past the KICS Grocery Store on the corner and along towards Hawthorn Road.

I was off to my first day at Hawthorn Road Infants School at 4 years and 4 months when suddenly the moment hit me! I really didn't fancy the idea and I objected strongly in the manner of many young children in similar circumstances, I cried long, very long and very loud!

We had reached the KICS Butchery Department at that moment, just above the Argyle Club and I was giving a fair rendition of a rain machine, there were tears everywhere. Undeterred however Mother pressed on, dragging her small charge around the Hawthorn Road corner, past Tom Croker's greengrocery emporium and a further fifty or sixty yards along to the Infant School gates. Still the tears flowed.

We had to enter through the school porch in order to register, along with all the other newcomers. This job eventually completed, with my tears still flowing, Mother left (very close to tears herself at my Oscar winning performance), whilst I was now in the very safe and most capable hands of Miss Evans. By mid-morning my tears had dried up, but I had set off numerous other newcomers, led by an even more prolific tear maker, Julie Loveridge, whose sobbing continued almost until lunchtime. What heroes those infant teachers were. I am not sure though how all their college training prepared them to be hit by many hours of copious tears from so many wailing infants during their working life.

However, the teachers certainly took their revenge, for after lunch they gave us all an oval rush mat, highly coloured I remember, which was placed upon the floor for us to fall asleep upon. Can you imagine attempting to sleep on a solid wooden floor with a rough corrugated rush mat prickling your arms and legs? I certainly wouldn't wish to try it now! Nonetheless we all managed to survive and we all actually turned up the following day and gradually, but slowly, progressed through the School.

It was during 1942, with World War II not going well for the Allies, that I made it from the infants, through the door that led into the hall, into the very first classroom on the right. Here Miss West reigned supreme. This was the Junior School. There were six other classrooms around the hall and one other on the first floor. I progressed gradually through the classes, year by year, Miss Cawston, Miss Wright, Miss Grudgings (she knew how to slap legs!), Miss Wagstaff and up the stairs to Mr. Payne. His classroom always fascinated me, but I never understood why. When the school celebrated its Centenary and held various events, I took my Mother along, who had been a pupil before me, and I just had to climb those stairs to enjoy a nostalgic moment or two in Mr. Payne's old room. It seemed so small to how I remembered it some 45 years earlier!

It was whilst in Miss Wright's class I remember that I had left my plimsolls at home and we were due for P.T. The order of the day was "bare feet for those pupils who have forgotten plimsolls". Now I had a problem, as I had rather dirty bare feet, (not continually, I should add, but merely on that particular day). Undeterred however and thinking quickly, I spat on my socks and gave the feet a good rub all over, cleaning carefully between the toes. Marvellous what a little spit would do! I felt a lot better for the "wash" and self confidence flooded back.

Carl Howard, age 9 years, 1946

Whilst cricketing in the school yard one lunchtime, the then Head Teacher Captain Hudson, when batting against the boys bowling, straight drove a good length ball high over the school wall bordering Hawthorn Road, over the road and straight through the

18

window of number 85, accompanied by a resounding smashing of the window pane, much to the delight of the pupils who had witnessed the drive with open mouths. However, in the time honoured manner of a school headmaster and commissioned officer of H.M. Rifle Brigade, Captain Hudson followed the ball across the road, rendered apologies in his best military manner, promised to settle the bill as soon as it was presented to him and then disappeared into the School, never to play cricket with the lads in the yard again.

Whilst in Mr. Payne's class I made what I suppose was my first claim to fame. We had a reading lesson and were to read against the clock. The target was 100 words per minute and I was the first pupil to break the barrier! Was I impressive? I certainly thought so!

As one last Hawthorn summer crept over us, Mr. Payne told the class that the school was to play cricket against Park Road School. The match was to be at the North Park, along Bath Road and I was to be captain. Quite why I was chosen I never quite understood, although I do remember responding to his question once asked, "*Where do Chelsea Football Club play their home games?*", with the little gem of "*Trent Bridge*". So, I suppose that I was half correct (correct answer Stamford Bridge). Possibly therefore I was captain through my superior sporting knowledge!

The day of the match duly arrived and the Hawthorn Road team took the field, hopes were high. The only other lad that I remember who played for us was Bobby Sims, who bowled left arm over the wicket. We batted first however, **totalling twelve runs**! Four was the highest individual score. There were two scores of two, thus leaving eight players and extras to accumulate four runs between them. Bobby failed to make an impact on Park Road, needless to say neither did anyone else and we were soundly thrashed! Matters were not made any easier for me when I was told, sometime later, that Johnny Worth had scored twenty four for Hawthorn in the corresponding game the following year. We could certainly have used him that afternoon in Summer 1948.

It was a little later that year that the top class sat the Eleven Plus examination, which would determine the pupil's future education. The options being Rockingham Road, Parish Church, Central School or High School for the girls and Stamford Road, Parish Church, Central School or Grammar School for the boys. Mr.

19

Laundon had shifted what seemed like hundreds of desks into the hall in great long rows, facing the famous, long serving George Harrison painting, that had hung at the back of the platform for many years. I remember sitting two thirds of the way back on the left, level with Miss Wagstaff's classroom, as we started our examination paper, brains whirring with deep thought as we stared into space and scribbled away alternately. Eventually time was called and our futures had been set and sealed. It seemed rather questionable that our futures could well depend largely on how we performed during that nerve wracking, palm sweating period in the hall, after six or seven years at school. Some of the girls who passed for the High School included Marjorie Slow, Margaret Green, Christine Edwards, Julie Loveridge, Diane Newman and Margaret Loasby, whilst Robert Smith, John Rowell and myself made it to the Grammar School. Roger Patrick passed for the Central School and became one of the best swimmers in Kettering. Sadly time fogs the memory about the remainder of the class.

I was nine or ten and had two great friends and school mates in Tony Braines and Jim Hickman, with whom I used to play after School. One day towards the end of the school holidays we decided to play in the deserted School playground. We were kicking a ball about quite happily when Margaret Panther walked by and made a comment to us about how 'out of order' we were. She was a year below me at School and I was never sure whether she lived in Argyle Street or Hawthorn Road, as when going home she used to disappear into an entry close to Tom Croker's shop in Argyle Street which served both streets. However, I have always felt that she put the boot in about our footballing activities, as a little later back at School, the word came down from on high that we three were required in the Headmaster's Office. Panic set in, the vision of the cane loomed. Shall I put an exercise book in my pants? No time, we were on our way! Mr. Bird advised us solemnly that he was fully aware we had been honing our soccer skills unofficially on the School premises, but merely warned us that he wanted no repetition and we were advised not to darken his doorstep again. I never did take up this case with Margaret Panther but, nonetheless I might yet have the opportunity one day.

As I mentioned earlier my Mother, Annie Musgrave, as she was in 1913 (aged 7 years when she started at Hawthorn Road) was a pupil for six years, according to her reference signed by Mr. Markham the then Headmaster in 1919. During the Centenary year she was invited to the school to tell tales of her schooldays to the children. Sadly I didn't really quiz her about them, but I do remember her telling me how much was made of Empire Day, which was commemorated on 24 May (Queen Victoria's birthday) each year. However, such celebrations must have fallen away during the 1940's. as I cannot remember any such activities during my schooldays.

It was to attend the reunions at the school Centenary during 1993 that I took Mother back to school again and she obviously thought that she would be the eldest ex-pupil to report in, as it were, as she was 87 at the time. We made the point to Richard Hall the Head Teacher who, to Mothers disgust, advised us that a young lady ex-pupil of 90 years had appeared the previous week!

Mother was not amused!

-- oOo --

During my 6½ years at Hawthorn Road School a number of young ladies attended from St. Gabriel's Home which was situated at the London Road end of Broadway. Some girls came for merely a brief period. One such girl was Sylvia Sadler (1946) who stayed only a few months until her foster parents came for her and took her to live in another part of Northamptonshire, too far away to continue at Hawthorn. Other girls attended for several years and indeed stayed at St Gabriel's until they were deemed old enough to go into the world to fend for themselves.

Children's Society Photograph

Roundhill Lodge for Girls, Kettering c.1906

21

Gabriel Court Residential Home, Kettering 2007

The Home was converted from a residential terraced house in 1905 and was then perhaps rather oddly named Roundhill Lodge. The Bishop of Leicester officially opened the building in April 1905. The four bedrooms were converted into dormitories and a laundry was built in the yard.

The name did not last very long as in 1908 it was renamed St. Gabriel's Home for Girls. Subsequently the neighbouring property was purchased and the address grew to 17-23 Broadway. The girls then enjoyed the benefits of a playroom, dining room, cloakroom, boot room, linen room and there was a sitting room for Matron and staff. In addition, there was a fair sized lawn for the girls to play on and also a yard where they took P.T. lessons.

During 1947 tradition went out of the window and The Home began to house boys.

St. Gabriel's Home however closed its doors in 1966 and then began a new life as an old folks residential home

In the very early days of St. Gabriel's it was administered by the Church of England Waifs and Strays Society which was renamed the Church of England Society in 1946.

-- oOo --

Throughout the years that I was at Hawthorn, during the 1940's, a huge oil painting hung in the hall at the back of the platform from where the Head supervised our morning assembly. I remember the painting as being probably four feet wide and some two and a half feet high, surrounded by a very elaborate gold coloured ornate frame.

It was painted by George Harrison, a local renowned Kettering artist. I have spoken to both Joan Carvell and Dorothy Webb, two of George Harrison's grandchildren, who revealed that George was "Kettering through and through", being born in Workhouse Lane (now Dryland Street) during 1876 and then living in Bath Road until he passed away in 1950. He was a hairdresser by trade, but also a skilled artist with a great interest in landscapes, and a talented writer and poet. He studied art in Brussels and afterwards was soon committed to cycling around his beloved Northamptonshire painting and sketching in the countryside. Granddaughter Joan told that he was particularly fond of the Welland Valley.

He was obviously a warm hearted man as he donated a painting of his to each of Park Road School, the Central School, Kettering High School, Rockingham Road School, of course Hawthorn Road School and also, to Carey Baptist Church.

The painting at Hawthorn had been taken down and stored for some considerable time, when it was decided that as there was no likelihood of it ever being put on show again, it would be auctioned at Bonhams of Market Harborough. Subsequently five or six years ago the painting was sold for between £900 and £1,000.

I did attempt to trace the purchaser through Bonhams, but to no avail, as I would have loved a photograph of the painting to show off within this book, a painting that had fascinated so many Hawthorn children over so many years during the 1920's, 1930's, 1940's and possibly even longer.

Unfortunately my quest was not helped by the fact that I couldn't even remember the title!

-- oOo --   -- oOo --   -- oOo --

NEW BOARD SCHOOLS AT KETTERING.

On Wednesday morning last a new block of Board Schools situated on the Hawthorne-road, Kettering were opened. The building which has already been erected forms part of a large scheme which will be completed later on, when the needs of the town demand it. At present accommodation is provided for 220 children. There is a room for infants, and a larger room, one part of which is to be devoted to infants of larger growth, and the other to babies. The large room is divided by a moveable wooden screen, so that the room can be thrown open for drilling and other purposes for which a large space is required. These rooms occupy what may be called the permanent part of the building. Attached to them is a temporary corridor and cloak room. These are built sufficiently substantial to serve their purpose for the number of years they will be required, but they are as lightly constructed as the Education Department will allow them to be, so that as little expense as possible may be required when it becomes necessary to pull down and rebuild. The rooms are 14 feet high, with the exception of the central portion, which is eighteen inches higher. The ceiling is flat, with a small cornice. The size of the small rooms is 24 feet by 24 feet, and the large room is 52 feet by 24 feet. The corridor is six feet wide, and the cloak room is 22 feet 6in. by 13 feet. In the completed scheme, the present front block will be lengthened at each end to contain the cloak rooms and entrance passages and masters' rooms, and there will then be accommodation for between 550 and 600 children. The whole building has purposely been kept very plain, and will depend for its architectural effect largely upon the grouping of the whole block when completed. The heating for the present will be done by means of open fires, supplemented by a certain amount of hot water piping, and provision has been made for a more elaborate system of heating on the completion of the whole building. The floors are of wood blocks, and the walls of brick with a painted dado and colour washed above. The parts of the walls that will eventually form part of the permanent corridors are lined with glazed brick to a certain height, and some of this is now visible on the outside, and looks, and will continue to look, rather meaningless until the completion of the building. The schools are almost entirely built of red brick with a red-tiled roof. An excellent playground is attached, and that part of it which will be permanent has been asphalted, the parts that will be covered by building at a subsequent date having been left bare. There is also an open play-shed, 45 feet by 15 feet, and plenty of detached sanitary accommodation. The architects are Messrs. Gotch and Saunders, Kettering; the contractor, whose tender for work amounted to £1,630, is Mr. G. V. Henson; the asphalt in the playground was put down by Mr. A. Barlow; and the iron fence surrounding the playground was constructed by Mr. H. Billson. It will be noticed that the work was carried out entirely by local men.

Kettering Leader and Observer Report – Friday 3rd May 1895

The World of Ice

Or, The Whaling Cruise of "The Dolphin"

And the Adventures of her
Crew in the Polar Regions

BY

R. M. BALLANTYNE

LONDON
BLACKIE & SON, Limited, 50 Old Bailey, E.C.
Glasgow and Dublin

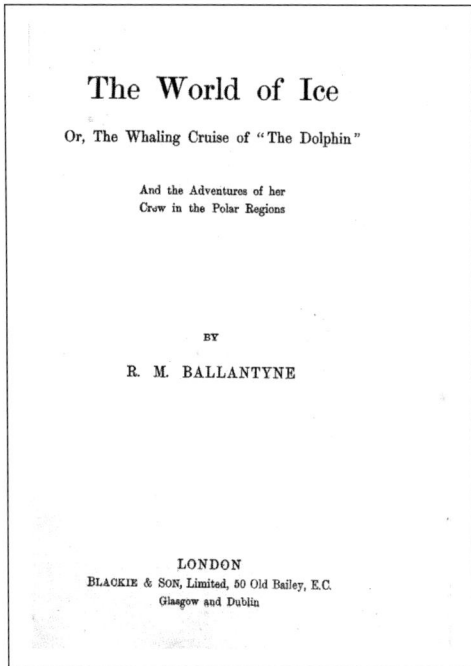

D.L. Photography

Tim Caswell's School Prize 1911

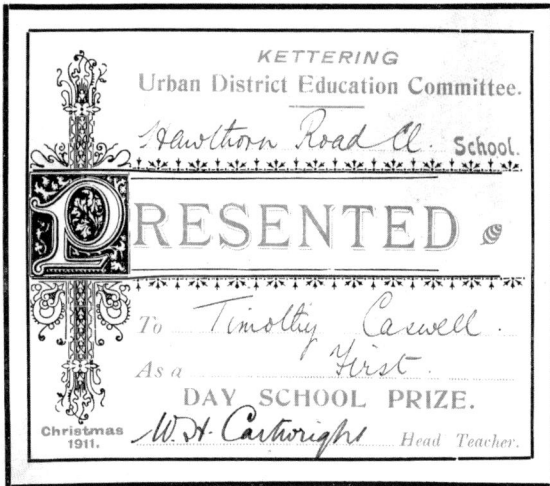

KETTERING
Urban District Education Committee.

Hawthorn Road Cl. School.

PRESENTED

To *Timothy Caswell*.

As a *First*.

DAY SCHOOL PRIZE.

Christmas 1911. *W.H. Cartwright* Head Teacher.

D.L. Photography

Certificate signed by W.H. Cartwright, Headmaster

D.L. Photography

Reggie Foster Certificates
Empire Day 1916
(See page 101)

D.L. Photography

Kettering Urban District Education Committee.

HAWTHORN ROAD JUNIOR SCHOOL.

Progress and Conduct Report.

Name _James Heaver_ Form _III_

No. in Form _38_ Position _1_ Average age of Form _4¼y_

Subject	Maximum Marks	Marks Obtained	Remarks
English	30	28	reading ought to be better
Arithmetic	10	6	
Geography	20	18	
History	20	18	Very interested
Nature Study	20	16	
Drawing	20	20	Consistently good
Handwork	10	10	
Needlework	—		
P.T. Country Dancing and Organised Games	-	-	Good leader.
TOTALS			

Regularity in Attendance _V.G._

Punctuality _V.G._ Form M

Conduct _V.G._

William Hudson Headmaster.

D.L. Photography

James Heaver Report 1937
Signed by Headmaster William Hudson

HAWTHORN ROAD COUNTY PRIMARY SCHOOL
KETTERING.

INFANT DEPARTMENT.

YEARLY REPORT.

Name .Isobel. Caswell........... Class ..1....

Age ...7.yrs.. 5 months....... Date .. July, 1955.

Reading: Very Good. Reading Age: 9 yrs. 10 mths.

Number: 92 % English: 92 %

Writing: Good. Practical Work: Good.

Conduct: Good.

General Remarks:

Isobel always works well and has made very good progress. She has shown much more confidence in her Number work of late and her test result is most promising. A very helpful, willing member of the class.

.....J. A. Taylor....
Class Teacher.

D.A.Woods.
Head Teacher.

D.L. Photography

Isobel Caswell Report 1955

How many children, how many miles?

THE ROCKING HORSE

Children stand with one foot in front of the other and knees slightly bent. They hold imaginary reins and rock backwards and forwards.

Rock - ing horse rocks me to and fro. Some-times fast, some-times slow. My

feet in the stir - rups, my hand on the rein, My rock - ing horse rocks me safe home a - gain.

Rocking Horse music

HAWTHORN ROAD
COUNTY PRIMARY SCHOOL

ANNUAL SPORTS

On Tuesday, 16th July, 1957

AT THE

Upper Headlands Playing Field
(By kind permission of the Kettering Borough Council)

BEGINNING AT 2 P.M.

HOUSE KEY

Buccleuch – B   Gloucester – G
Dalkeith – D   Montagu – M

PROGRAMME 4d.

D.L. Photography

Annual Sports Day Programme 1957

EVENT 21. 80 YARDS—Under 10 Boys
R. Stapleton B   C. Shorley B   A. Adams D   D. Hirst G
J. Watson G   R. Brooks M   R. Fennelow G   P. Smith D

EVENT 22. 80 YARDS—Under 11 Girls
M. Norman B   J. Peasgood B   H. Dickerson B   J. Elmore D
M. Thrift G   B. Pringle M   H. Howlett M   J. Goulding M

EVENT 23. 80 YARDS—Under 11 Boys
M. Pook B   G. Woolsey B   P. Perkins D   S. Exton D
R. Burdett G   B. Jellis M   M. Pettiquin M   C. Langer M

EVENT 24. 100 YARDS—Under 12 Girls
V. Cleaver B   W. Holmes B   A. Eastbrook B   M. Clark M
U. Smith G   P. Underwood G   J. Gower D   E. Shaw M

EVENT 25. 100 YARDS—Under 12 Boys
R. Morgan B   J. Wilcox B   J. Savory D   G. Whymant D
D. Baird G   T. Miller G   D. Whymant G   J. Hatsell G
C. Claydon G

EVENT 26. MOTHERS RACE

1   2   3

EVENT 27. SCOTCH HORSES—Boys Under 7
J. Mann & M. Buttner   B. Ward & T. Mobbs
P. Hudson & C. Betts   R. Whitlock & R. Franckam
S. Whymant & S. Shatford   R. Watkins & A. Holditch

EVENT 28. SCOTCH HORSES—Under 8 Boys
S. Goulding & R. Moore   P. Stowe & S. Brooks
H. Ainsworth & P. Laud   A. Irons & R. Miller
G. Malsher & P. Ford   R. Springthorpe & G. Piggott

EVENT 29. THREE LEGGED—Under 9 Mixed
J. Towell & R. Arden   B. Butlin & M. Sims
R. Seville & M. Foreman   J. Campbell & D. Cole
S. Ambrose & I. Dent   C. Pritchett & Rich. Clark
P. Sharpe & M. Mellish   J. Brading & C. Rouse

EVENT 30. THREE LEGGED—Under 10 Mixed
G. Dunkley & L. Baxter   B. Stubbs & M. Savory
J. Mason & J. Larcombe   R. Devlin & I. Caswell
A. McAlwane & C. Stokes   H. Cleaver & H. Small
R. Ellis & A. Adams   P. Vadler & John White

EVENT 31. THREE LEGGED—Under 11 Mixed
E. Gardner & J. Cook   M. Mason & R. Lindley
H. Howlett & A. Baxter   H. Roberts & M. Thrift
M. Campbell & M. Stewart   M. Pook & P. Pettiquin
R. Burdett & S. Exton   M. Norman & J. Goulding

EVENT 32. THREE LEGGED—Under 12 Mixed
S. Gore & A. Eastbrook   A. Nobles & C. Steggles
J. Knight & M. Jackson   M. Clark & N. Holmes
J. Gower & D. Wood   S. Webster & S. McGee
B. Pettit & C. Gunstone   D. Whymant & T. Cunnington

EVENT 33. SACK—Under 9 Boys
J. Lawrence B   C. Butler B   C. Pritchett B   P. Sharpe D
Robt. Clarke G   R. Smith G   C. Rouse M   M. Fillingham M

EVENT 34. SACK—Under 10 Boys
John White B   R. Stapleton B   N. Burden B   P. Jones G
J. Ives M   D. Hirst G   J. Watson G   R. Brookes M
P. Vadler M

EVENT 35. SACK—Under 11 Boys
E. Cleaver B   G. Woolsey B   M. Pook B   C. Noble B
S. Exton D   R. Burdett G   K. Davis M   C. Langer M

EVENT 36. SACK—Under 12 Boys
B. Morgan B   T. Miller D   J. Savory D   T. Robinson D
D. Baird G   C. Claydon G   K. Allen M   J. Hatsell G

EVENT 37. FATHERS RACE

1   2   3

EVENT 38. WHEELBARROW—Under 9 Mixed
J. Towell & R. Arden   M. Sims & B. Butlin
M. Hogan & D. Cramer   M. Foreman & R. Gould
V. Stapleton & D. Cole   R. Clarke & C. Pritchett
J. Campbell & R. Franckam   P. Sharpe & M. Mellish

EVENT 39. WHEELBARROW—Under 10 Mixed
H. Cleaver & T. Gaulden   A. McAlwane & C. Stokes
M. Savory & B. Stubbs   L. Baxter & J. Larcombe
C. Shorley & C. Walker   R. Fennelow & B. Foster
D. Hirst & R. Stapleton   M. Watts & P. Malsher

EVENT 40. WHEELBARROW—Under 11 Mixed
M. Mason & H. Roberts   J. Peasgood & M. Norman
B. Simpson & P. Wallis   J. Elmore & D. Cramer
S. Oakden & M. Thrift   M. Pook & P. Pettiquin
E. Cleaver & R. Genry   J. Whitlock & S. Exton

D.L. Photography

1957 Sports Day Programme inside pages

PRIZE WINNERS 1958

CLASS 1.
1st. Susan Hegarty. 2nd Jane Whitworth.
3rd. David Butler.
Progress: Brian Sharrocks, Elizabeth Tingle, Jean Watts.

CLASS 2.
First Year: 1st Pamela Furnell. 2nd Jonathan Mann.
Second Year 1st Richard Lund.   2nd Margaret Towell.
                ⁻Progress: Richard Moore, Christopher Turner.

CLASS 3.
1st. Peter Stowe. 2nd. Alan Panter. 3rd Robert Springthorpe.
Progress: Susanne Jewers, David Wrighton, Christine Taylor.

CLASS 4.
1st. Charles Rouse. 2nd Helen Rhind. 3rd. John Lawrence.
Progress: Sheila Martin, Richard Ford. Neil Markham.

CLASS 5.
Third Year: 1st. Paul Wilson. 2nd Jean Sharrocks.
Fourth Year:1st. Suzanne Smethers. 2nd. Kathleen Daniels.
Progress: Anthony Hales.

CLASS 6.
1st. Robert Ellis. 2nd. Alan Thompson.3rd.Christopher
Shorley.4th. Nicholas Burden.
Progress: Isobel Caswell. Hazel Cullum.

MERIT PRIZES.
Allan Dawkins, Eileen Hogan, Karolyn Higgins, Mary
Phillips, Christine Stylianou, Clive Walker.

NEEDLEWORK AND CRAFTWORK PRIZES.
Vivien Cole, Ruth Jones, Rosalie Frankcam, Jean
Larcombe, Peter Ford, Philip Lund, Richard Jahn,
Richard Brooks.

D.L. Photography

1958 Prize Winners Speech Day

Prize Giving and Speech Day Programme 1959

From pupil to teacher

NATIONAL CYCLING PROFICIENCY

CERTIFICATE

Awarded To

NICHOLAS ANDIC

who has been trained to cycle safely and passed the NATIONAL CYCLING PROFICIENCY TEST as approved by the Minister of Transport, the Secretary of State for Scotland and the Minister of Home Affairs, Northern Ireland.

Certificate No. 14142/1

Date 7.7.64.

President
The Royal Society for the Prevention of Accidents

D.L.
Photography

Nicholas Andic Cycle Proficiency Certificate and Prefect Badge
1964

Chapter Four

Evacuees and School Outposts

Bernard Hales Photography

Pollard Evangelical Church today
Previously known as London Road Hall

DURING World War II the school opened its doors to the evacuee children pouring out of London in order to get away from the Luftwaffe and the regular air attacks. The first mention we find relating to these children within the school records, is an entry for 28th September 1939 (which was a mere 25 days after our country declared war on Germany) indicating that a Mr. Drury, the local sanitary inspector, had called to examine stocks of Evacuee Emergency Rations and sad to relate he had to remove unsuitable tins of meat! The second reference was on 10th November 1939 when the school nurse arrived to inspect all the evacuee children.

During the early 1940's the School had many, many visits from various London sources, all concerned with the welfare of the evacuees. I did, however, have quite a surprise whilst researching the school "Call Book", as during November 1940 three visits were made by Colchester School Inspectors to check upon their evacuees. So the evidence indicates that Hawthorn Road School helped out evacuees from both London and Colchester during World War II.

Unfortunately I am unable to include an estimate of the numbers of evacuees taught at Hawthorn Road School, but provision was made for teaching accommodation within St. Edwards Catholic Church Hall in The Grove, behind the Catholic Church; the Toller Sunday School Rooms in Meeting Lane at the side of the Toller Church and also within the London Road Hall (now Pollard Evangelical Church) which is opposite to the St. Mary's Hospital grounds.

Bernard Hales Photography

St. Edwards Church Hall, The Grove, Kettering. Classroom during World War II

25

Whilst I was at school, between 1941-1948, I remember being taught in St. Edwards Catholic Church Hall. My class used to alternate with the evacuee class, in that we worked mornings one week and the evacuees would work afternoons. The following week we would change around.

Yet when Ron Ashby (1935-1942) was at school, he was taught at the London Road Hall and also at the Toller School rooms on an alternate morning/afternoon arrangement, in classes that included evacuees.

Sybil Allen (1935-1942) believes that the school had a whole London school, sharing the facilities whilst she was at Hawthorn.

In addition to London Road Hall, Toller School rooms and St. Edwards Church Hall, the facilities of the cricket pavilion in Lewis Road were also used, as yet another annexe to the school from September 1941.

The Lewis Road sports ground, which is situated off Pytchley Road, was owned by the Kettering Industrial Co-operative Society (KICS). Cricket and football were played there in the 1930's and into the early 1950's. Part of the ground has now been taken over by the Southfield School for Girls, but the remainder stays much the same today.

Judy Derry (*nee* Russell) and Eveline Godson (*nee* Williams) tell of their two years in the infants classes at the Pavilion School (as it was known) in Chapter Seven of this book. Mick Cotton, who became a renowned County tennis player was also taught there. The first thing he remembered was the leaky roof!

-- oOo --

Although Elm Bank Hostel held no actual direct connection with the school, I feel it would be remiss not to mention it within these pages.

Elm Bank is situated in Northampton Road on the hill, just before the road turns towards Northampton.

The Hawthorn evacuees who were housed there during the 1940's and 1950's appeared to be those children who could find no home within the community and Elm Bank provided an alternative.

Numerous Elm Bank children attended Hawthorn for several years and their names, together with the name of the Hostel, are to be found within school records for varying reasons during and just after the years of World War II.

The Hostel became a nursing home after the evacuees had gone, many years ago. Whilst now, having been empty for some time, it looks quite sad, boarded up and with weeds growing everywhere, planning permission is sought to knock down the buildings on the large site in order to build flats (August 2007).

-- oOo --   -- oOo --   -- oOo --

Chapter Five

Contributions from Pupils and Staff – Times gone by

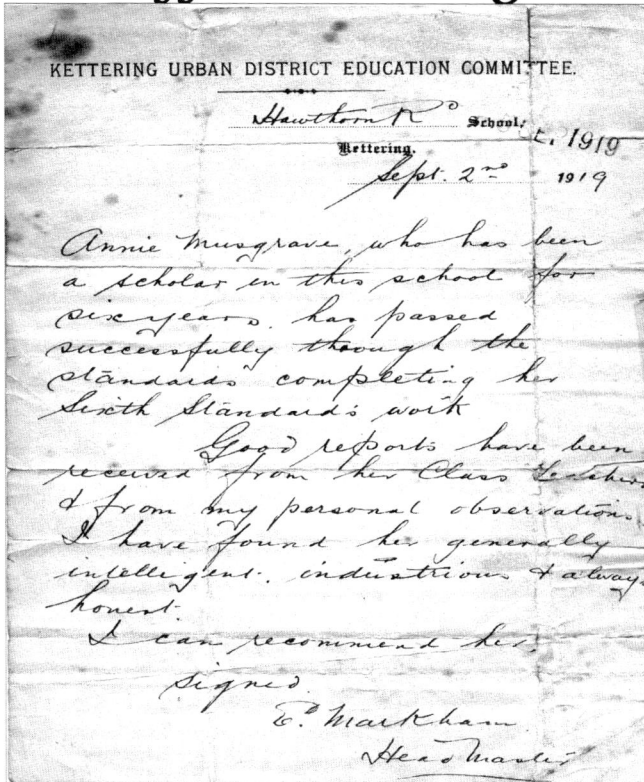

KETTERING URBAN DISTRICT EDUCATION COMMITTEE.

Hawthorn R___ School,
Kettering.
Sept. 2___ 1919

Annie Musgrave, who has been a scholar in this school for six years, has passed successfully through the standards completing her Sixth Standard's work.

Good reports have been received from her Class Teacher & from my personal observation. I have found her generally intelligent, industrious & always honest.

I can recommend her.

Signed.
E. Markham
Head Master

D.L. Photography

Contributors to this Chapter

Percy Saddington	1895 – Not known
Eva Horan	1928 – 1935
Len Foster	1930 – 1936
Barbara Caswell	1931 – 1938
Beatrice Bruce	1933 – 1939
Sybil Allen	1935 – 1942
Ron Ashby	1935 – 1942
Shirley Torlott	1935 – 1942
Elvin Royall	1936 – 1942
Joyce Luck	1937 – 1943
Brian Reynolds	1937 – 1943
Norma Hilliard	1938 – 1944
Brenda Bridgstock	1939 – 1945
Margaret Watson	1939 – 1946; 1970 – 1987
Ivor Sumpter	1942 – 1948
Roy Ashby	1945 – 1952
Bernard Hales	1946 – 1952
Martin Turner	1947 – 1954
Richard Wardle	1947 – 1950
Richard Barlow	1949 – 1956
Isobel Caswell	1953 – 1959
Nicholas Andic	1956 – 1962
Eddie Giacobbe	1959 – 1965
Susan Clarke	Early 1960's
Janet Deer	1960 – 1965
Barbara Smith	1960 – 1967
Steven Robinson	1965 – 1970
Philip Maddison	1966 – 1973
Richard Wright	1971 – 2002
Jane Watson	1989 – 2005
Maureen Eaton	1991 – To present

I have gratefully received many reminiscences for this Chapter from past pupils (N.B. prudently not referred to as 'old pupils') and staff of varying eras.

I do feel that in some cases, time has possibly fogged the memory somewhat, as contributions did not always hang together when the same incident was being described by different pupils. Except in unusual circumstances I have included at least part of each submission from all past pupils. In these circumstances therefore, I feel that I cannot be held responsible for the whole truth or otherwise of these recollections, but I would suggest that the reader should be prepared to accept a little journalistic license with certain contributions. With this in mind, therefore, I offer the following paragraphs for your delectation. Each contribution is led off with the name of the student whilst at school, together with the period over which their education covered which, in some cases, is a "guesstimate" due to the passage of time!

-- oOo --

Percy SADDINGTON (1895-?)
It was during May 1976, whilst 86 years of age, that Percy appeared again at Hawthorn. He first appeared as a pupil during 1895 (or possibly 1896), just after the school opened. The E.T. carried his story upon Percy's return to Kettering to see old friends, when he told of being in the school hall, saying prayers for those in the Boer War (1899-1902). Percy had left Kettering during 1939 and had moved to St. Leonards-on-Sea.
What made his situation quite remarkable, was that Mr. and Mrs. Dee of London Road (with whom Percy had stayed whilst at Kettering) told me that he was completely blind and he had travelled by train all alone to Kettering.

Kettering Evening Telegraph

Percy Saddington said prayers for the soldiers in the Boer War whilst he was at Hawthorn. This visit was during May 1976

30

Eva HORAN (1928-1935)
Eva tells of when she used to live at 31 Pytchley Road, close to Captain Hudson and family. She used to walk to school, hand-in-hand with Peter (Captain Hudson's son) for several years, as they were in the same class together through the infant school. *"They were happy times"*, she recalls, *"and I remember Miss Anstey our infant teacher, she was lovely!"*

-- oOo --

Leonard FOSTER (1930-1936)
Relates that his father, Ralph who was born in 1900, attended the school along with brother Reg and sisters Gertie and Blanche. Len lived directly opposite the infants entrance.

He remembers one year when the family went on holiday to Mablethorpe, they had hired a well fitted out railway carriage to stay in and to his horror, as he watched from the carriage a 1906 green Austin motor appeared in the distance and gradually drove closer and closer. He knew of one person only who had such a vehicle, Mr. Moule, the teacher from Hawthorn Road – sure enough Len was correct, as Mr. and Mrs. Moule had booked the carriage next door. What a way to start a holiday!

Later on, Len was playing soccer at the Headlands playing field in a school period and was tackled by a teacher. The tackle broke his ankle. He fancied that he would be good for a week off. The next day however as he was still in bed, a party was sent over to carry him into class. So much for living too close to school – there was no slacking in 1935!

He well remembers the enthusiasm with which Empire Day was celebrated. In fact, a huge red-gold flag from Kettering Tasmania was hung in the hall and apparently Hawthorn Road School had sent a Union Jack to Kettering Tasmania as a reciprocal gesture. How and why the flag exchange came about sadly is not known however.

-- oOo --

Barbara CASWELL (1931-1938)
Barbara, along with her three sisters Joan, Jill and Janet and father Tim, were all pupils of Hawthorn Road School and she tells of how much everyone appeared to so enjoy their school days. She

31

fondly remembers Captain Hudson, the Headmaster and Miss Butler the Deputy Head who also taught piano. Barbara used to dislike however playing at school concerts, particularly the duets with twin sister Joan playing together on the same piano, at Miss Butler's insistence.

She also tells of the St. Gabriels girls and indeed fondly remembers one such girl (name sadly forgotten) who joined the Caswells at their home for Sunday afternoon tea on various occasions.

-- oOo --

Beatrice BRUCE (1933-1939)
Tells of being a St. Gabriels girl for the period whilst at Hawthorn Road School. She tragically lost her mum very early in her life and spent her formative years in (her words) a happy, wonderful, environment at St. Gabriels in the company of up to 30 girls. Eventually going on to Parish Church School, having been told that she wouldn't be sitting her 'Eleven Plus' as there were no funds to purchase uniforms, sports kit etc. should she or any of her contemporaries pass the entrance exam for the High School or the Central School. Following her secondary education, at the age of 15, a vacancy occurred for a staff member at the Home. Beatrice successfully applied and in fact worked in the Broadway Home until she was 22 and about to be married.

She well remembers the Hawthorn Road School Headmaster of her time, Captain Hudson, who being a truly professional commissioned officer, rejoined his World War I regiment following declaration of World War II.

-- oOo --

Sybil ALLEN (1935-1942)
I quote from Sybil's e-mail:

I remember in 1939/40 that until they built air raid shelters in the playground we had to see whether we could run home within a given time if the sirens went. – I then lived in Netherfield Road. Fortunately I don't think we ever had a real air raid warning. Teachers were called up, Mr. Moule came out of retirement I think to take over the headship (to my relief as I disliked his predecessor). I particularly enjoyed being taught by Miss Grudgings. We

32

had to share the school with one evacuated from London and often had classes at other venues e.g. Toller Chapel rooms off Gold Street and the Chapel opposite St. Mary's Hospital.

We always had to walk round the edge of the polished floor in the school hall except when we had country dancing classes which I enjoyed. Mr. Laundon was the caretaker and had the unenviable task of cleaning up after any of us who were sick.

-- oOo --

Ron ASHBY (1935-1942)
Ron remembers the St. Gabriel's girls well – one such young lady more so than the rest! When the class used to walk in crocodile fashion from the school to the Headlands playing field, Ron confesses regularly to being at the end of the crocodile, as he and his tall, thin, young lady friend used to move sharply into the brick air raid shelter that had been built on the grass verge in the Oval, for a very quick kiss!

"She was taller than I was", he relates, *"so I had to stand on my toes."*

Diplomatically, as befits a true gent from Hawthorn Road School, Ron fails to remember his young lady friend's name.

-- oOo --

Shirley TORLOTT (1935-1942)
Remembers:

Headmaster Captain Hudson; deputy Alan Payne; infant teachers Miss Dixon and Miss Anstey; junior teachers Miss Wright, Miss Cawston, Mr. Moule, Miss Hamburger and Miss Whitworth.

She well remembers also the school assembly with hymns and prayers each morning – free milk (in 1/3 pint bottles) which was warmed on the radiators in winter and drunk through real straws (everyone chose fat ones)! There was physical training, known as "drill" in the yard in good weather, otherwise in the hall. The class would be divided into four groups, each group being distinguished

33

by the wearing of a red, yellow, green or blue band draped across one shoulder.

She tells that there were three separate playgrounds: infants, boys and girls. There were open fronted shelters at the far end of each, with a bench along the back and each side. The toilets were close by, at the furthest point from the school building, so pupils had to run across the yard in all weathers following an affirmative response to the "Please may I be excused Miss ?" request.

During the late 1930's an inter-school event took place on a field at the southern end of Kettering, known as "the 40 acre", later built on to become Highfield Road. It is believed the occasion was that of Kettering becoming a Borough (*Note: Kettering became a Borough in 1938*). A marching drill display featured in this event.

On Empire Day Headmaster Captain Hudson, who had served in World War I, held a very long assembly during which he related very poignant and often bloodcurdling stories to an under 11 year old audience. The children sang patriotic songs and hymns and then had the afternoon off.

Once a week the class played musical instruments, drums, castanets, triangles and tambourines and very positively called the ensemble a percussion band. Again once each week there was a country dancing class and the class performed to such tunes as "Picking up the sheaves".

The timetables comprised mostly half-hour segments on sums, reading, writing, drawing, history and geography with mental arithmetic being the exception being allocated 15 minutes only.

-- oOo --

Elvin ROYALL (1936-1942)

"School Memories at Hawthorn Road School"
My first school was just around the corner from where I lived. Most of the pupils lived within a short distance of school and had to walk there. One of my earliest memories, is of waking up at night during a thunderstorm. My father came to comfort me and we watched the lightning from my bedroom window. Suddenly there was a

blinding flash as the school 'chimney' was struck, and the loud report of thunder came instantaneously.

I think it was during my first week at school, that we had a story read to us on a Friday afternoon. There we were sitting on the wooden floor in a semi-circle listening as the story unfolded, intent on every word, not daring to move in case we missed a sentence. The story was just coming to an important point, when I became aware of a spreading circle of warm water! I had to go to find the caretaker so he could clear up the mess. When I reached the classroom door and turned the large brass knob to open the door, I looked back to where I had been sitting and a pool of urine was on the floor. The girl I had been sitting next to, still sat there, with her head propped up by her hands, listening to the story I was now going to miss.

Later in that first year I was feeling ill, so I was allowed to stay away from school. When time of the mid-morning break was near, I must have been feeling somewhat better, and was in the garden with my pedal-car one moment and at the school gate just as the other children came out to play, the next. They saw me there and dashed down the playground to ask how I was feeling. I remember going to school in the afternoon!

I was still at the Junior School when my father changed his job and we moved house. I still went to the same school, which meant about a mile walk from the town four times a day, in all weathers. It was during this time that war was declared and the headmaster was called up into the army. One day after lunch I had got about half way to school when the air raid sirens went. I ran the rest of the way to school with one eye on the skies overhead on the lookout for German planes. The rest of the children were already in the underground shelter when I reached school and joined them, sitting on the wooden slatted seats that receded into the darkness.

The Evacuees, or Vaccy's as we called them, arrived and caused a total disruption to our school life. They had the sole use of our school in the mornings and we had to go to a church hall, one week. The next week it was the afternoons and we had the school in the mornings. The

35

school day was also disrupted, first by the introduction of double-summer time, which brought the clocks forward by one hour even in the winter time and then the school day was started at 8.30. It was like getting up in the middle of the night.

The winter of 1940 was cold, with snow and ice, even the lake at Wicksteed Park was frozen solid. The thing that made early morning school bearable was the hot, fresh baked bread bun bought from the bakery just across the road from the school. Held to the ears brought relief from the cold wind for a moment, then take a bite and scoop out the hot soggy dough with a finger. This left the warm, crisp crust to be eaten before it was time to enter class. One day I had missed the roll in the morning so I bought a cold one at lunch time. It was not the same, cold bread loses its appeal somehow.

Each classroom was heated by an open coal fire, with a brass topped fireguard to keep eager children away from the flames. The milk came in small bottles which were frozen in the winter with the cardboard top perched on a pinnacle of frozen cream. To make the milk drinkable it was placed in front of the fire to thaw out. The cardboard circles with a hole in the middle were used as a base for woollen pom-poms in art classes, even though they gave the finished article an aroma of sour milk.

When I first went to school the Headmaster was Mr. Hudson, after War was declared he was called up and came back to say goodbye as Captain Hudson in Officers uniform. The new headmaster was Mr. Moule.

The winter of 1940 was very cold, Wicksteed lake was frozen over and people used to skate on it. The children having split shifts at school often went to the park during the day. I went one morning and decided to break the ice on one of the smaller boating ponds. The ice had been smashed around the edges for the ducks and then it had glazed over during the night. I jumped on the ice to break it and my wellington boot went through the surface and I was up to my knee in icy water. I took my boot off and emptied the water out, took off my sock, which I put inside my mac, put my boot back on again and headed home.

36

When I stood in front of my mother, I undid the belt of my mac with a flourish, the sock fell out hitting the floor with a clunk, it was frozen solid!

Certain historic events happened whilst I was at Hawthorn Road School, which were marked by presentation mugs. George V died just around a year after his 25th Jubilee when I was taken to Wicksteed Park for the firework display which ended with a representation of the King and Queen. 1937 was marked by the intended Coronation of Edward VIII. Followed by the Coronation of George VI. Two mugs in one year! The main streets were hung with red, white and blue tinfoil decorations. The next year another mug and the same decorations for Kettering becoming a Borough.

The one thing I remember about my journey to school were the railway wagons and horses resting outside Piccadilly Buildings opposite to the Library. They would leave the station about 8.30 a.m. struggling up the sharp incline. If I was early they would still be coming, usually they were having breakfast with the drivers resting in the shop doorways eating sandwiches wrapped in newspaper. If they had gone on their way to deliver the goods stacked on the wagons, I knew I would be late. It would be a hard run all the way to school. The Headlands was lined with trees and in the autumn I would shuffle through the fallen leaves. There were conkers to gather for use in the playground.

(Elvin Royall's work was e-mailed to me during September 2007 and was received with grateful thanks. C.H.)

-- oOo --

Joyce LUCK (1937-1943)
Phoned to say that she remembered Hawthorn Road as a very happy school. The only teachers recollected were Miss Anstey and Mr. Moule.

-- oOo --

Brian REYNOLDS (1937-1943)
Tells that he can only remember the Headmaster, Captain Hudson and Miss Cawston from the teaching staff. He does however remember the huge painting that hung on the wall behind the Headmaster in the school hall.

"I hope that's still about", he said (See Chapter 3)

-- oOo --

Norma HILLIARD (1938-1944)
Norma remembers sleeping on the famous rush mats in her first year. Following three years in hospital and thus absent from school, she remembers the care and help afforded to her by Miss Grudgings when she eventually returned. She also recalls the 40 get well letters received from her classmates which were sent to the hospital bedside. All 40 said the same thing, word for word. Norma was rather suspicious and thought that possibly, just possibly, Miss Grudgings had the class copy the letter from the blackboard! It was a lovely thought though!

-- oOo --

Brenda BRIDGSTOCK (1939-1945)
Brenda tells of the small bottles of milk that the children had mid-morning. The bottles had small cardboard lids with a push through hole in the middle for the straw. The children used to take turn being milk monitor, putting in the straws and giving out the milk. The bottle lids were kept and used as frames to create woollen bobbles.

At one time the pupils were only having half a day schooling each day as room for the evacuee children had to be made whilst they were away from their homes. Brenda couldn't remember how long this arrangement continued.

All the pupils took a gas mask to school and practiced to see how fast they could get into the air raid shelter, which was in the playground, just in case of a bomb scare. It was thought all good fun and the danger certainly wasn't recognised.

-- oOo --

Margaret WATSON (1939-1946; 1970-1987)

"Hawthorn Remembered"
Early years. *I have been associated with Hawthorn Road Primary School since 1939, first as a pupil, then as a member of the teaching staff.*

One of my earliest recollections of the Infant Department was when my mother had given me one penny (1d) to spend on some sherbet sweets. Unfortunately for me, I was discovered by my teacher eating them in class, and was told to "put them in the waste paper basket". I went to the basket, but I had enjoyed them so much that something inside me said "No", and I pushed them under my jumper and kept them there for the rest of the afternoon!

Following the Infant Department I progressed to the Juniors, where I must have received an excellent all-round education, for I passed the 11+ examination a year under age, and went with due ceremony to the Kettering High School for Girls, and from there to London University's Furzedown College.

***Music at Hawthorn**. My appointment to the staff at Hawthorn came in 1970, where I was responsible for the teaching of music in the junior school, following the retirement of Miss Grudgings. The Education Authority had recently enlarged its peripatetic music staff in order to give instruction on a weekly basis in violin playing. With this support, I formed Hawthorn's School orchestra of some 60 players, training the children to play the full range of recorders, together with the glockenspiel, percussion instruments and the most popular instrument of the day, the guitar. I arranged well-known songs from the charts, like the Osmonds' 'Love me for a Reason' and Don McLean's 'American Pie' to be played by this combination of instruments and the popularity of the orchestra went from strength to strength with pupils of all ages and abilities vying with each other to become a member. After playing at the Kettering Schools' Music Festival, where the orchestra received an enthusiastic reception, the Music Adviser for the county, **Malcolm Tyler**, asked me to become the Secretary of the Festival Committee, following*

39

*in the footsteps of the redoubtable **Miss Gladys Riseley, M.B.E.** a well-known and respected figure in local music circles. I was honoured to take on this important role, which I continued to do for many years, and through this position I was able to be in contact with other music teachers in Kettering and the surrounding district. When many of them asked me to teach them to play sufficient chords on a guitar, so that they might imitate Hawthorn's musical success, I willingly did so, teaching a large group on a weekly basis at Hawthorn School, until they became proficient in playing the basic chords and their inversion. The orchestra's reputation quickly spread in other circles, via encouraging articles in the local Evening Telegraph newspaper, and the children were invited to play at garden fetes and to give concerts at senior citizens' retirement homes for their parties and other functions. These were indeed halcyon days in the Hawthorn Road social calendar.*

***The Butterfly House.** This project was another innovation which quickly gained the interest and enthusiasm of the children. The house was similar to a horticulturists polytunnel, (closed at both ends!) with a double safety door for the children to enter. They were shown how to produce butterflies and moths from eggs, through the larvae and chrysalis stages to the adult insects. The appropriate food plants were grown in the house for all the different larvae the pupils had access to, and they were responsible for keeping the plants fresh, and for recording changes from egg to adult butterflies and moths. One insect which caused an enormous amount of interest was an Indonesian Moon Moth, which had a wing span of approximately 30cm. It was so large that some of the younger children were afraid to go into the house; they felt safer viewing it from outside the tunnel! Again, the E.T. showed encouraging interest in the project, and apart from writing an article about the Butterfly House, they included a photograph of the Moon Moth, (with its wings obligingly outstretched!), resting on the hands of one of the children. The interest shown by the children in this work encouraged me to make a video 'Butterflies in my Garden', showing the kinds of moths and butterflies they could expect to see, and the kinds of food plants to grow in order to attract the insects. Together with the video was a folder* *of worksheets, containing further information, and arranged in the form of puzzles, crosswords, word searches and games. When assisting in music courses at Grendon Hall and other venues, I would show the video to the children in their free time, and encourage them to do the worksheets. It was most encouraging to note the enthusiasm and interest the video created, and **Dr. Miriam Rothschild**, the world renowned expert on moths and butterflies, wrote, in a Foreword to the video:*

The excellent video illustrating British Butterflies should make the children's visit to the garden both exciting and instructive. I hope the thrill and interest of their experience will last them all their lives, not merely be forgotten as part of school lessons.

(Signed) Miriam Rothschild

Ashton Wold   *3 February 1996*

The work came to the attention of the authorities at Sywell Country Park, and I was invited to assist in the creation of their butterfly garden. When it was opened, children from Hawthorn were especially invited to attend, and they also visited the Stratford butterfly house, and the one in London, giving truth to the old adage 'from little acorns....'.

Headmasters and Colleagues. *No recollections of mine would ever be complete without reference to the Headmasters and colleagues whom I remember with great fondness and affection, and from whom I received unstinting help and support in all my activities and projects throughout my teaching career at Hawthorn Road.:*

Headmasters **Woods and Findlay**, *whose interest in music and musical theatre led to the school productions of The Wizard of OZ, Oliver and Annie. (Peter Findlay's portrayal of the character of Fagin in 'Oliver' may never be surpassed on the amateur stage). All these productions were artistically designed and produced by* **Paul Aucott**, *and invariably played to capacity audiences.*

Bob Scotney, *whose friendship, help and support will remain as a dear memory of my time at Hawthorn Road*

41

School. His organization and running of the Parents' Association's Autumn Fair raised valuable funds for the School's activities.

***Miss Everett, Mrs. Gerrard, Mrs. Smith and Mrs. Ashby**, all respected and loved teachers in the Infant Department all helped to initially engender an interest in music for their pupils by organizing singing games, dancing and percussion work.*

***Mrs. Tidball**, whose needlework skills made a valuable contribution to the success of many school productions.*

***Mrs. Manning** and **Mrs. Garton**, who in the canteen provided excellent hot mid-day meals for hordes of hungry children.*

*Finally, to **Miss Mary Bonham**, whom I invited to come to the school after her retirement as Instructor at the Kettering Swimming Pool, to teach the younger children to swim, an invitation to which, in typical Miss Bonham fashion, she readily agreed.*

I enjoyed my teaching career at Hawthorn Road School, and the memories I have of the children I taught, and of the staff with whom I worked, will always remain very dear to me.

(Margaret Watson presented me with her memories during August 2007 and I take great pleasure in producing them in full as above – C.H.)

-- oOo --

Ivor SUMPTER (1942-1948)
Remembers that on his first day at school he walked home to Boddington Road at morning playtime as he thought that school had finished for the day. He used to stay for school dinners (at the price of 4 old pence each) and following one such lunch was wiping his lips with his handkerchief when the other children on the table started laughing at him, as they always used their sleeves. Another lunchtime when he was sitting with older brother Brian and great friend Arthur (Archie) Naylor of Summerfield Road, the trio could not face their lunch at all, the hard potatoes and lumpy custard

were just too much. The food therefore was tipped on one plate and stirred rather well. Nevertheless when the dinner supervisors, Miss Cawston and Miss Grudgings saw what had happened, the unfortunate trio had their heads tipped back so that the food could be spooned into their mouths. After all it was so wrong to waste food in war time!

Ivor also tells of the school children being marched to London Road en-bloc to greet King George VI as he passed by in his limousine. He can't really remember the occasion though. It was thought possibly to have been 4th March 1943 when the King and Queen toured the Kaycee Clothing factory in Field Street, followed by a drive to Wellingborough to visit the Ultra Electric factory.

-- oOo --

Roy ASHBY (1945-1952)
Tells brother Trevor that he remembers teachers Miss Wardle, Miss Everett, Miss West, Miss Grudgings, Mr. Lee, Mr. Burkhill and Mr. Wignall. His Headmaster was Mr. Bird and the school caretaker Mr. Laundon

He recalls sampling various shades of punishment whilst at Hawthorn. The cane across the hand from Mr. Bird, a slipper on the rear end from Mr. Wignall and a slap at the top of the leg from Miss Grudgings. He also remembers receiving 'lines' from a number of teachers.

Roy tells of playing school football with John Ritchie (see Chapter Eight) whose twin brother James was in the same class. Apparently Roy and John were the team full backs – John had an attacking role, whilst Roy stayed in defence. Chris Sharman was their goalkeeper and the team shirts during that period were pale green.

-- oOo --

Bernard HALES (1946-1952)
Remembers transferring from the Pavilion School in Lewis Road (which was a converted sports pavilion) to the main School when Mr. Bird was the Headmaster:

He goes on to say:

"I remember Miss Grudgings who used to pull up our short trouser legs and smack us if we had done something wrong!

From what I remember I was frightened of all the teachers – there was certainly no playing the teachers up.

School milk was given to us twice a day and a class member was appointed milk monitor for a week at a time.

The memory of school meals – the cabbage smell that came from the kitchen I still remember!

From my reports I seemed to have been a satisfactory pupil but I took my eleven plus at the school and failed it!"

-- oOo --

Martin TURNER (1947-1954)

Remembers canings that went on during his time at school. He recollects one lad who came back to class with blisters on his hand and another boy who pulled his hand away just too late to prevent his finger nail being ripped off.

"Unbelievable", he says, *"it certainly couldn't happen today!"*

-- oOo --

Richard WARDLE (1947-1950)

E-mails the following lovely little story:

Mildred Wardle was my aunt, and would have taught at the school from approx. 1943-1946/7.

A little anecdote about Mildred. She taught Roy Ashby my cousin (Hawthorn Road 1945-1952) and he was also of course her nephew. One day she made Roy "stand behind the blackboard" for misbehaving. She went home to the Crescent at the end of the school day and Roy's mother said "Where's our Roy?" Mildred: "Err....oh dear he must still be behind the blackboard!" (he was all alone locked in the school).

Aunt Mildred died in 2004 aged 87, cousin Roy lives in Derbyshire aged 66.

-- oOo --

Richard BARLOW (1949-1956)

Richard phoned to tell the story of 1952 when he designed the school blazer badge, a sprig of hawthorn with white blossom. His good friend Jimmy Woodburn, who was a far better artist than Richard, tidied up the design and the Hawthorn badge was born.

Richard also tells of his first day at school, when the lovely Miss Everett put out her arms to stop him leaving the classroom. Richard took a large bite of her arm and years later during the Centenary celebrations when Miss Everett discovered to whom she was speaking, she pulled up her sleeve and showed Richard, to his horror, the scar that he had left so many years before!

-- oOo --

Isobel CASWELL (1953-1959)

Tells of a young girl named Rhona Punch from Trinidad who came to Hawthorn Road School during 1958 for a six month period to stay with her relations in Hillside Avenue. The two young girls became firm friends and indeed quite recently Rhona found a note, when her mother passed away, which was written by Isobel's mother asking if Rhona could come for tea after school one day. Rhona returned to Trinidad following her six months at Kettering, but the girls kept in touch by letter and later by e-mail. They met up again briefly in 2001 when Rhona travelled to London with her daughter. Subsequently Isobel flew to Trinidad for a holiday with her great friend, who at one time she hadn't seen for over forty years, but remarkably had continued what was obviously a tremendous friendship that had blossomed from the main hall at Hawthorn Road School so many years ago.

Miss Dunmore's class of 1955 showing Rhona Punch third row from the front on extreme left.

-- oOo --

Nicholas ANDIC (1956-1962)
Was the eldest of five siblings who graced the classrooms of Hawthorn Road School during the 1950's and 1960's. One of his most memorable reminiscences was regarding teacher Bob Scotney's habit of lighting up and smoking a cigarette whilst teaching the class! Nick also reveals that he has a fine collection of School photographs, prefect badges and Sports Day ribbons which his mum used to keenly and proudly collect.

-- oOo --

Eddie GIACOBBE (1959-1965)
Grateful thanks to Eddie for a very interesting letter and I feel that I would do him an injustice should I not produce it in full. See below:

Hi Carl,

Apologies for the delay in sending the photos I mentioned, hope you find them useful, they are still in reasonably good condition considering how old they are.

Eddie Giacobbe Collection

Miss Everett's class of 1959

"Eddie is front row sitting extreme right, investigating Chris Jones left ear"

I was at Hawthorn Road School from 1959 to 1965 and at that time I lived in Windermere Road, Kettering – my parents have lived there since 1959.

Amongst my recollections of the school are of course the daily 1/3 pint of milk which we all liked and if we were lucky we would get a second bottle if there were any left.

We also had school dinners too in those days – no fast food rubbish – but pretty wholesome if quite dull food, we used to pay 2/6d per week for school dinners.

There was also a swimming pool and I think we were probably one of the first schools in Kettering to have one – it was an outdoor pool – not heated and we had to shuffle through a tray of disinfectant before getting into the pool. I remember using polystyrene floats whilst we were learning to swim.

I can also remember playing for the school football team. At that time there was a local schools league – we used to play our home games at the Headlands playing fields and I remember one season we had lost every game until the final game when we beat Avondale School 3-1. It was regarded as such a triumph that we were given a special mention in assembly the following morning by Mr. Woods the Headmaster.

One thing I remember is that on the morning of a game – we would eagerly stand around the school notice board to see if we had been named on the team sheet then we would go to the stage in the main hall and our kit would be waiting for us all neatly piled – shirt, shoes and socks. We played in Green and Yellow Quarters, the shirts were like rugby shirts with collars, heavy material and the socks were heavy woollen, the shorts pretty much came down to our knees.

Some years later my football career was to get a real lift when I had a series of trials with Northampton Town and in fact I was there when the Cobblers lost 8-2 to Man. United in the FA cup – George Best scored six that day – I think it was 1971/1972. I never made it as a player – but

47

went on to enjoy many years of playing at local league level until I was 48!

I remember listening to BBC schools radio broadcasts in class and also there was a programme called 'Music and Movement' which was basically PE with dance and music.

I remembered the annual school games at the Headlands every summer and we were encouraged to take part in many events and if you won a race you would receive a red ribbon as I recall. Mr. Woods the Headmaster was a nice man – fairly strict – his wife also taught at the school and I believe they eventually retired down in the West Country. Mr. Woods was always looking to raise funds for the school and there were annual jumble sales/Christmas Fayres etc.

The Christmas concert was an annual attraction and I can remember the stage being set up for this – dark grey curtains and home made lights, nothing too technical, it was all very basic but we had a lot of fun.

I also recall us being treated to a full length feature film or cartoons in the main hall – this usually happened at the end of term before the summer break.

Very happy memories – I'm sure more will come to me – but for now I hope this will be of some assistance to you in your research.

Regards

E. Giacobbe

Eddie Giacobbe

-- oOo --

Susan CLARKE (early 1960's)
Fondly remembers Mr. Woods who just loved school events, some even to raise funds of course. She tells of the Autumn Fair, with

Miss Everett masterminding the White Elephant Stall, films in the hall, shows by travelling actors, the harvest festival, country dancing, Christmas plays, sports day, prize giving and super Christmas parties, which always produced hotly contested fancy dress competitions.

The school houses were Dalkeith (yellow), Buccleuch (green), Gloucester (blue) and Montague (red). The uniforms were bottle green and grey blazers, the girls had a beret with a Hawthorn badge, whilst the boys had a cap and green flashes on grey socks.

She remembers the stories under the trees in the playground during warm weather. The Blenheim Orange apple tree remains today. The canteen brings mixed memories! (lamb with wobbly fat-ugh!). She also remembers the outside toilets!

In fact Susan loved the school so much, that she returned as Sue Eden, teaching staff, 1989.

-- oOo --

Janet DEER (1960-1965) – School Clerk
Janet writes that she was one of the first school clerks within the county. She really enjoyed her work and she was part-time initially, working four hours per week, which developed towards the end of her service (through the school being such a happy place with seldom any trouble) to an 8.45a.m. to 3.30p.m. affair when she was coming in and going home with Gareth and Josephine, her two children, who were pupils at Hawthorn Road. The extra hours were her choice entirely, as there were certainly no extra wages for her!

She had great respect for the Headmaster, Mr. Woods, described as a "*sweet gentleman*", who set the tone for the whole school.

Quite whether Mr. Woods felt sweet and gentle, when the school suffered a very bad attack from head lice, which affected virtually all pupils and the staff, including the Headmaster, is not known! Janet, for her part, even passed her 'nits' on to her husband!.

Rather a smiley story now, but I am certain that it wasn't thought so at the time!!

-- oOo --

Barbara SMITH (1960-1967)
E-mails that she was a second year infant in Miss Everett's class
and remembers that some six years later (after Barbara had left
the school) she saw Miss Everett walking her dogs one day and she
looked exactly the same then as when she taught her – she had
obviously discovered the secret of eternal youth! Barbara also
remembers the swimming pool being built during the early 1960's
and what's more she remembers that the water was absolutely
freezing cold all the time!

-- oOo --

Steven ROBINSON (1965-1970)
E-mails that he used to live in Windermere Road and his mum
used to walk him to school each day and return later to collect
him. He maintains it was *"one hell of a trek for a 4½ year old, and
his little legs got shorter by the term!"*.

-- oOo --

Philip MADDISON (1966-1973)
Says that one thing he will always remember was that Mr. Woods
was a bloody good shot with the board rubber and also liked the
slipper!!!

-- oOo --

Richard WRIGHT (1971-2002) – Teacher of stringed instruments
Served the school for one day each week in his musical capacity,
which was backed up by his experience with the Royal Marine
Band. Worked under three headteachers, Messrs Woods, Findlay
and Richard Hall. During his time of over thirty years with
Hawthorn Road School, colleagues particularly remembered were
Mike Coleman (Deputy Head), Margaret Watson (Music), Mrs
Barney (Infants), Paul Aucott (Drama), Arthur Idle (Special Needs)
and Bob Scotney. Pupils remembered though the quality of their
music included Mark Perrott, Ross Watson (bass guitar) and
Michael Smart (violin), who later became a Doctor of Medicine.

-- oOo --

"The School Secretary"

Secretarial staff were first introduced to Hawthorn School in the mid-fifties. Before this the Head Teacher would complete all the clerical work himself and all documents were hand-written.

The school secretary's duties would have included general correspondence, filing, collecting dinner money and other monies arriving at school for trips and purchases, keeping pupil records and registrations up to date and helping with sports days, fayres and the like. A manual typewriter was purchased for her use and later a stencil duplicating machine was used for reproducing copies of letters to pupils and programmes. She would only have worked for two or three hours a day, although this increased as more responsibilities were passed to the school office.

This is a far cry from today's secretary who is now expected to act as a bursar and has the use of electric typewriters, word processors, computers, photocopying machines and other modern technology. The hours of work have also increased greatly to keep pace with the extra duties and now there is a full-time Secretary/Bursar and part-time clerk at this school.

1988 proved the time when the biggest change to the school administration took place with LMS being introduced into schools and therefore more responsibility and work coming to the Head Teacher and inevitably the administration staff. The Head Teacher, working with the Governors, now manages the school's budget and all orders, invoices and banking duties are dealt with in the school office. The hand-written ledgers were replaced with computers and software packages to enable the school and the LEA to monitor the budget and ensure the money was being spent as agreed by the Head Teacher and Finance Committee of the Governors.

Training was given to those involved with the new technology and there is a good support help line if any difficulties are experienced, but the job has certainly grown away from the "easy little job that fitted in with the

51

children's holidays". The status of the secretary has now risen and she is considered on a professional level, although her duties are so numerous with some very mundane, but important jobs, still being undertaken. At Hawthorn the administration duties include the following:

Receptionist/ Telephonist
Head Teacher's P.A.
Secretary to all staff
Bursar (including day to day working with the budget, orders,
    invoices, payments, banking, etc.)
Filing Clerk
Keeping pupils records up to date (both on the computer database
    and record cards and folders)
Keeping personnel records up-to-date (on computer database)
Liaison with parents, governors, the LEA and suppliers
Dealing with returns and forms to the LEA
Handling, recording and banking of all monies for sales, trips, fund
    raising, photos and other small items
Supervising reprographics
Looking after sick children (until parents can be contacted)

The list is endless as many other jobs are also done from time to time to help out the staff, children, parents and others involved in the school. The great variety of work makes the position both interesting and rewarding with a feeling that the secretary is helping with all aspects of the school life.

("The School Secretary" was written during 1995 as part of Jane Watson's Advanced Diploma in Professional Studies in Education. Jane filled the position of School Secretary at Hawthorn from 1989-2005 and very kindly allowed me to use her work, within this book, for which I am most grateful. C.H.)

-- oOo --

<u>Maureen EATON (1991 – the Present)</u>
Maureen tells that she has Hawthorn connections as far back as 1979, when her son attended the School, later followed by his two younger sisters. She extended these connections in 1991 when she became a dinner lady during the days that the School lunches came from a central kitchen and were dealt out from a huge metal container on wheels. Later of course, times changed, cooked meals finished and the children resorted to sandwiches brought from home or in the case of a few where parents were on state benefit, were provided by the School. At this point Maureen's job title changed to that of "lunchtime supervisor".

"A posher job title but the wages stayed the same", she revealed with a smile.

She remembers a great day out that was enjoyed with her daughter's class during 1992 when a visit was made to Stoughton Farm Park near Leicester which was a small farm attraction (owned by the Leicester Co-operative Society) which sadly has now closed. The children can be seen in the trailer, just prior to a tractor driven tour of the Park!

Maureen Eaton Collection

A trailer load of trouble at Stoughton Farm Park. 1992

-- oOo --   -- oOo --   -- oOo --

53

1905 Datestone with original School entrances.
'Infants' – 'Boys '– 'Girls' may just be seen at the top of each respective archway.

The Chimney with adjacent window from the east, constructed 1905

Kettering Urban District Council headstone

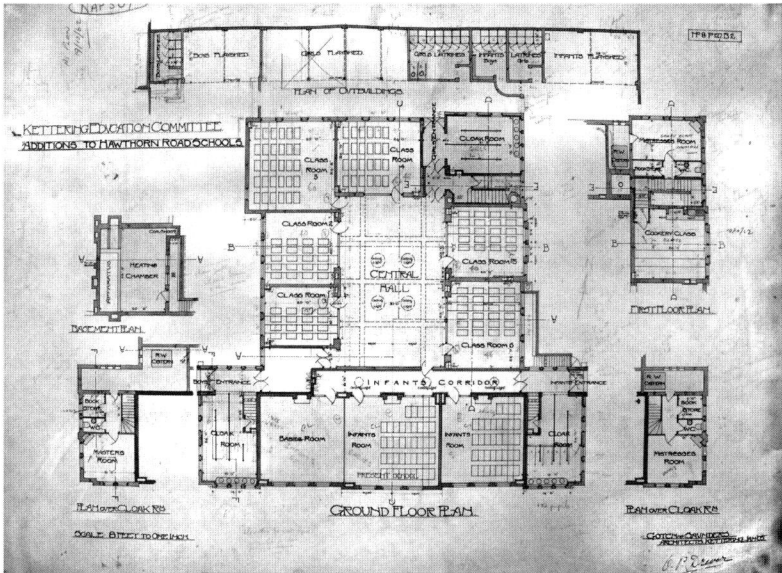

1905 Ground floor plan
Architects drawing

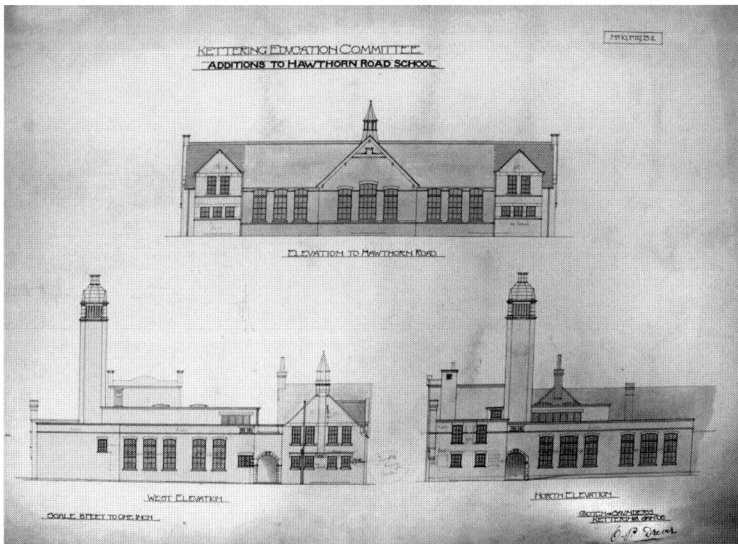

1905 Elevations
Architects drawing (note builder O.P. Drever's name in bottom right corner)

Barbara Law

Boys Dance (or P.E. Class) in Hall 1911

Richard Wardle

Horse and dray, (belonging to Richard Wardle's Grandfather) of Jacquest and Wardle, outside Hawthorn C1912

Richard Wardle

Richard Wardle's fathers class 1921
Richards father is back row 3rd from right

Nora Cheatle

Standard 2. 1926

Back row: Vera Litchfield, Joan Redhead, Margaret Chambers, Nora Cheatle, Audrey
Gunn, Kathleen Green, Dorothy Croker, Pat Tait
Second row: Norah Parnell, Ella Baker, Doris Dalby, Rose Willis, Betty Roe, Marjorie
Hallam, Margaret Elmore
Third row: Peter Bolton, Geoffrey Timson, Norman Thompson, Norman Claydon, Henson
Wright, Victor ?, Cyril Butcher, Leslie Litchfield
Front row: Leonard Houghton, Joseph Fairey, David Greaves, Harold Rollings, Jim Law,
George Parnell, Ivor Arber

Miss Jarvis's class 1933

Party time youngsters 1935
Roy Peach, Betty Cooper, Michael Stretcher, Hazel Sumpter, Violet Foster and June
Porch may be seen within the group

School Soccer Team 1937-1938 – Taylor Cup Winners
Rear row: Mr. Payne, John Wesson, Paul Taylor (Cup donor – Taylors Cycle Shop,
Montague/Silver Street corner), Jack Taylor, Lawson Bowman, William Hudson –
Headmaster
Centre: Don Snape, Terry Wright, Eric White
Front: Dougie Underwood, Fred Barrett, Terry Asher, Nip Collyer, Tony Bradley and Eric
Bland

School Soccer Team 1946
Top row: Mr. Burkhill, John West, Joe Waters, John Petts, Neil Stevenson, John Ashby,
Mr. Payne
Middle row: Derek Balding, John Cooper, Mr. Hudson, David Creamer, Arnie Dorr with
John Hilliard behind
Front row: Brian Old, Ginger Smith and Mick Eady

Mary Ashby

Teaching staff c.1944
Top row: Mildred Wardle, N/K, N/K, Miss Wright, Miss Grudgings, Mrs. March, Miss
West
Front row: N/K, Miss Wagstaff, N/K, Mr. Moule, Miss Cawston, Miss Evans, Miss Everitt

David Needle

Speech Day 1950-51
Mrs. R. Tailby (Mayoress) presenting David Needle with his prize. The teacher is Mr.
Smith and the lady to his right is the Headmaster Mr. Bird's wife.

Christmas Party 1954 with Pam Betts (Centre) – as a Christmas tree

Harvest Festival 1954 with the George Harrison painting, centre, rear

Harvest Festival 1959 – with Miss Grudgings and Mr. Burkhill supervising

Harvest Festival 1959 – Three winners for sure!

Mary Ashby

The School Orchestra 1973

Mr. and Mrs. Woods look well following retirement in their Dartmouth Home C1975

School staff of the Millenium

Mike Coleman

School Class 1 - 2005

Jacc Batch

Chapter Six

Do You Remember?
Reminders of School Days

Mr. Burkhill (second left) with Councillor C.W. Godfrey, teachers Irene Grudgings and Miss Everett with an unknown school girl – December 1962

WHILST researching the Kettering School Board minutes, the School Log Book, Punishment Book and Call (Visitors) Book, (kindly lent to me by Richard Hall), along with various copies of the Evening Telegraph, for suitable items for this Chapter, it came home to me that the school had developed as a pillar within the local community, by virtue of the many, many sides to its character. Year after year, especially at Christmas time the school children had visited St. Mary's Hospital, Burton House and Ferndale Old Folks Home for example, in order to entertain the sick and elderly. From school Harvest Festivals up to 250 parcels were distributed annually to the local pensioners. The children had shared their choral mettle and musical repertoire with the public within other schools and local churches. Indeed during December 1983 the music group, including recorders and singers, presented a special item in the Parish Church Carol Service.

Mary Ashby Collection

Mrs. Margaret Watson can be almost seen in the bottom left of the photograph taken at Ferndale Old People's Home.(early 1970's)

Interest had no doubt been acquired in public performance by virtue of the enthusiasm of certain staff members, together with the aid of travelling entertainers who, over many years, had been welcomed to the school. The Robert Cooper Theatre Company; Argyll Theatre Group; Kettering Gold and Silver Band; Northants Music School; Da Silva Puppets; Ivan Scott, with Spanish guitar; and the Seagull Theatre Players were but some of the visiting thespians who had whetted the appetite of the children. The various school leaders were owed much credit (and indeed still are) for developing this side of the pupils education, helping them to become both mentally and practically stimulated children.

The many school outings created great interest and again it is of much credit to the staff, that time and trouble were taken to organise the children into what at times were huge parties to convey and supervise to such diverse places as Barmouth for a four day visit with 33 children and 3 staff, to the Science Museum and Planetarium in Central London, to Peterborough Cathedral with 73 juniors, 3 staff and 2 other adults. To Whipsnade Zoo, Bekonskot, Windsor, Stratford-upon-Avon, Hendon RAF Museum, Bath, Tower of London, Hampton Court and most importantly many visits within our own County were organized – the Triangular Lodge at Rushton, Naseby Battlefield, Guilsborough Grange, Stoke Bruerne, Pitsford, Brixworth, Foxton Locks, Rothwell Church and crypt, and Lamport Hall – all were visited over the years by many, many Hawthorn pupils.

Horizons were further widened from the late 1950's with the regular staging of the Harvest Festival, the Autumn Fayre, plays and concerts, the drama and music festival, prize giving, sports day and exhibitions of craftwork. Models, lampshades, mats, rugs, skirts and dresses were made, displays of P.T., charities were supported and of course the very first Swimming Gala 1972, were all fitted most successfully into a hectic curriculum. In fact whilst pursuing this additional character building, one wonders where the time was found for the pursuit of the "three R's". Nonetheless examination results proved that **"Reading, 'Riting** and **'Rithmetic"** were by no means neglected!

However, back to my research for various dates of items of school interest. Some of the entries that I found are shown below in strict chronological order. A number of these are possibly hard to believe, but be assured dear reader, each item is as found in official records!

-- oOo --

29 April 1895:   Mrs. Cooper of Hawthorn Road, to be appointed Caretaker, being paid £2 per month. (*NB. Mrs. Cooper was still being paid £2 per month in January 1904*).

56

25 March 1898:	Mr. Boyles employed to sweep chimneys.
28 February 1925:	The Clerk reported that F.B. Jowett had presented the school with a water colour entitled "Polperro Harbour" and it had been hung in the school hall.
28 January 1932:	Peter M: Sticking his pen point into girls and boys in his class and wasting blotting paper – 3 strokes across the buttocks.
28 June 1932:	Gordon K: Syringing latrine water over other children – 3 strokes across the buttocks.
3 September 1935:	Vincent D: Sly cunning misbehaviour – 2 strokes across the buttocks.
6 November 1936:	Miss Goulsbra called re. rubber shoes for P.T.
21 December 1936:	The expected number on roll after Christmas would be 471.
29 January 1937:	Mr. H. called to complain about the treatment of his daughter.
28 July 1937:	Councillor Walter Dyson called to hear the percussion band.
4 February 1938:	Two Government officials called and decided that Hawthorn could accommodate 120 beds in time of emergency.
4 March 1938:	Two police officers called re. damage to a house in London Road.
25 November 1938:	Members of the Education Committee called to see the electrical heating apparatus at work.
13 January 1939:	Mrs. Rowles called re. Betty's gloves.
7 July 1939:	Mrs. Goodliffe and others called re. children

57

being allowed to go on the busmen's outing to Skegness.

28 September 1939: Mr. Drury, Sanitary Inspector, called to examine remaining stocks of evacuee emergency rations and ejected unsuitable tins of meat.

1 October 1939: Miss I. Grudgings commenced duty.

10 November 1939: School Nurse called to inspect L.C.C. children.

6 February 1940: Mrs. L. called to beg shoes for her two absent children.

4 March 1940: Wm. P., Ronald A., Tony T., Edward E., Leonard P., Peter D.: These six boys reported to have been the leaders in some rough horseplay outside the London Road Hall and being the ones to incite a dog to bite younger children before any teacher was on duty – 1 stroke on each hand.

21 March 1940: Mrs. K. called re. Olives head.

26 April 1940: Miss Tilley called to bring bill for sweets supplied at Christmas.

27 June 1940: Mr. Osborne H.M.I. to inspect A.R.P. trench progress.

24 July 1940: Nurse Ryding called to complete inspection of heads.

28 August 1940: Mr. Woodhead H.M.I. visited to see school shelters and note numbers of London children.

20 September 1940: Mrs. I. called re. vermin in Jill's head.

1 October 1940: Miss Price called, being a Welfare Visitor for Colchester group.

58

18 December 1940:	Mrs. Turner called to have a milk paper signed.
17 January 1941:	Colchester teacher called to check up on evacuees.
14 February 1941:	James M. spoiling the contents of about 60 milk bottles – 4 strokes on the buttocks.
13 March 1941:	Miss Goulston called to see London Road Hall.
8 April 1941:	Mr. Cheatle called to discuss fire watching in connection with local street party.
2 May 1941:	Miss Speakman called for lists of 60 evacuees and to confer re. cases needing attention.
20 May 1941:	Mrs. C. reported that Iris had no shoes.
5 September 1941:	Mr. Hudson called with Peter.
23 September 1941:	Miss Ewington called re. evacuees scabies.
30 October 1941:	Miss Gailston called to visit Toller School and Grove School.
22 January 1942:	Sergeant White called to beg a bit of chalk for military purposes.
15 May 1942:	Surveyors Department officials called re. black out.
4 June 1942:	Mr. Swannie called to question some "Elm Bank" boys.
15 June 1942:	Mr. Woodhead H.M.I. called to check iron railings for proposed removals.
8 October 1942:	P.C. Hunt gave talks to children at Hawthorn, Grove and Pavilion Schools.
22 January 1943:	Mr. Williams – Sybil's father from London

59

called to enquire about clothes and forms.

4 February 1943:	Mrs. P. and Mrs. B. called re. childrens verminous heads.
18 February 1943:	Mr. Wills called to inspect black out arrangements.
20 September 1943:	Miss Henson reported interference with her apples.
2 February 1944:	A.R.P. warden visited to test childrens gas masks.
15 February 1944:	Police Sergeant called to collect ammunition etc.
2 November 1944:	Mrs. Davies called re. forms for clothing coupons.
23 March 1945:	Ronald S., Walter B., Brian C, Ivor S., Brian S., - disobeying teacher in charge at dinner duty. These boys went wandering into the streets against orders – 1 stroke on the hand.
20 June 1945:	Dentist and assistant: Inspection of all children at Hawthorn Road School, Grove and Pavilion.
5 June 1951:	Richard C: writing on lavatory wall – 3 strokes on buttocks.
10 April 1972:	School re-opened after Easter Holiday. 542 children on roll.
14 June 1972:	3rd year infants able to use the pool for the first time this year.
27 September 1972:	Infant School Harvest Festival. Rev. Ruddick of the Parish Church was the guest speaker. 120 parents present. More than 200 parcels of produce were sent out to deserving old folk at the end of the day.

15 December 1972:	Service of lessons and carols in the afternoon when a party of old people were school guests. The 4th year children looked after them very well indeed, refreshments were served after the service in the canteen; and following on, presentations were made to teacher Mrs. Tevendale and cook supervisor Mrs. Manning to mark their retirements.
16 May 1973:	Swimming pool used for the first time this season.
30 June 1973:	The School Orchestra, under the direction of Mrs. M.P. Watson played at a Garden Party at Ferndale Old Peoples Home. This was well supported by parents and children.
3 July 1973:	Several of our children took violin examinations under the Associated Board.
20 December 1973:	Annual juniors Christmas party, fancy dress competition, films, tea. Noisy but much enjoyed. Evening reception for Mr. and Mrs. D.A. Woods who retire 31 December 1973. Mr. Woods will have served as Headmaster for 20 years and 1 term. His successor is Mr. P.A. Findlay from St. Mary's C. of E. School, Kettering.
4 April 1974:	Mr. Keeling came to school with four of his animals. His talk was very popular with staff and children.
29 October 1974:	A party of 92, 3rd and 4th year children together with the Head, Mr. Scotney, Mrs. Watson and Mrs. Findlay visited the BBC T.V. Centre to see a recording of the BBC "Record Breakers" – with Roy Castle.
6 January 1975:	School opened with 436 pupils for the Spring Term.

7 February 1975:	A number of 4th year children are taking ski-ing lessons at Rushden in the evenings, accompanied by Mr. Scotney and Mrs. Watson.
15 March 1975:	Our girls netball team won the Northamptonshire Netball Championship by beating Falconer's Hill in the final by 5 goals to 4. A very thrilling morning.
16 January 1976:	As the girls, led by Mrs. Watson, left Highfield School after netball, a shot was fired over their heads. Police informed.
9 April 1976:	Presentation of a gold watch to Miss Everett, a splendid teacher who has given 30 years service to Hawthorn in a career spanning 40 years.
19 May 1976:	We had a visit from Mr. P. Saddington, now resident at St. Leonards-on-Sea. He came to Hawthorn in the 1890's, commencing school at 3 years old – he spoke to 90 children of the 4th year.
13 May 1977:	The following boys won their football badge: Denis Jackson, Andrew Kyte, Saul Frampton, Colin Brooks and Michael Pask.
30 June 1977:	Town Sports. Our girls retained the "Under 12's Relay Cup". Miss Bonham retired after 41 years at Kettering Swimming Baths.
13 December 1977:	Mr. D.A. Woods (previous Headmaster) reported that he and his wife are now Deputy Mayor and Mayoress of Dartmouth.
26 April 1978:	The Headmaster presented netball "colours" badges to Alison Reid, Julie Adams and Oriel Andic.

*The 1977-78 School Netball Team
Rear: Cindy Caulton, Julie Hayley,
Georgina Pett, Claire Ingyon, Berenice
Liggins,: Joanne Bell Front: Martine
Steel, Alison Reid, Oriel Andic
(Captain), Julie Adams, Sarah Gardner*

22 June 1978:   A great evening concert for people from the Henley Centre with our orchestra, choir and individual performers.

2 October 1978:   During the weekend the school was broken into. Three netballs were stolen, eight internal windows were smashed and five classrooms were devastated by vandals. The police were informed and a detective, together with a photographer/finger print expert, came to school at 7.45 a.m.

16 February 1979:   Deep snow with drifting made travelling practically impossible. Very few children turned up – only about twelve – so school was closed for the day.

6 March 1979:   At noon half a house brick fell from the chimney stack on next door house – overlooking boy's playground. The stack looks unsafe. The house is empty. Phoned the estate agent.

13 October 1979:   After much excellent pre-fair work by Mr. Scotney, parents and teachers, an excellent Autumn Fair produced a wonderful £700.

27 March 1980:   Richard H. – bowling bricks at flowering daffodils – 3 strokes on the buttocks.

8,9,10 December   We presented "The Snow Queen" on these

63

1980:	three evenings. The theatrical experience of Mr. Aucott and myself plus the musical expertise of Mrs. Watson and the wholehearted support of the staff and many parents have made this a really superb production. It is the finest I have been part of in my career and that covers many excellent shows (Peter Findlay).
6 March 1981:	An immense tragedy for our school. Our dear Mrs. Gerard died suddenly. She collapsed during the night and died in the Intensive Care Unit at the General Hospital. The staff is grief stricken, the children stunned.
18 June 1981:	Chess badges awarded to Robert Clarke, Jason Smith, Timothy James.
2 September 1981:	School opened with 240 children on roll.
13 November 1981:	Six members of the Northamptonshire Music Schools' Wind Group gave an enjoyable recital this morning.
28 May 1982:	Visit from a 65 piece German Youth Band from the Johannes Gymnasium in Lahnstein. It was a wonderful 50 minute concert which was received with cheers and roars of applause.
11 June 1982:	A splendid educational outing to Warwick Castle with the 2nd year.
13 July 1982:	Today is open day. We have Maypole dancing and country dancing. I am presenting 35 Cycling Proficiency certificates. The Sports Personality of the Year is Lisa Golland. "Service to the School" cups go this year to Karen Smith and Claire Byrne. The classrooms were open with "School Outing" themes (Peter Findlay).
16 October 1982:	The Autumn Fair was held today and the

64

remarkable sum of nearly £900 was raised.

22 October 1982:   This afternoon we welcomed many guests including Mr. Stan Smith, Mrs. Gerard's brother, Mrs. Ginns, Chairman and members of the Governors, friends and acquaintances of Mrs. Gerard, parents, staff and children. I spoke a few words about Mrs. Gerard and then all present were able to see the seating area with flower tubs and hanging baskets which we have built and arranged in memory of Mrs. Gerard, who died in March of last year.

D.L. Photography

Whilst Hawthorn School exists, I hope that each Headmaster who follows me will always keep this area as a memorial (Peter Findlay).

1 September 1983:   School opened with 255 children on roll.

13 October 1983:   Seagull Theatre presented "Peer Gynt" in the school hall. Staff and children enjoyed the performance.

15 November 1983:   3rd year – Chiropody examinations.

12-14 December 1983:   We presented our junior play, "The Adventures of Orphan Annie". Over 100 children took part and five members of staff joined the cast. Mrs. Watson responsible for the music and Mr. Scotney for lights. A

65

great team with much help from parents and friends. The reception of the play reverberates among parents and around the town. Produced by Paul Aucott it was without doubt a triumph.

5 April 1984: Today was a busy day! The interviews were held for the Headship of the school from 1st September. The successful applicant was Mr. R. Hall from Farndon Fields, Market Harborough. It was the highest powered panel to be assembled for a school other than comprehensive. Congratulations to Mr. Hall – I hope that he will have as much success and happiness as I have had in the last 10½ years – (Peter Findlay, Headteacher)

6 June 1984: David Prowse, T.V.'s Green X Code man visited school.

17 December 1984: School Carol Concert held at United Reform Church, London Road.

21 January 1985: The decorators began work today. It is generally believed to have been at least 20 years since the school was painted.

15 May 1985: Party visited Oxford to see production of "Joseph".

20 December 1985: School Carol Concert held at Toller Church. Attended by large parent congregation.

8 March 1986: Sponsored swim involving 6 children – James Read, Ivor Eaton, Simon Odell, Alison Richards, Catherine Labram and Emma Morley plus school secretary Mrs. June Smith. Approx. £400 raised on behalf of British Heart Foundation.

30 September 1986: Class 6 (Mrs. Maner) visited a fishmonger.

2 October 1986: Harvest Festival. Each class presented an

66

item to a packed and appreciative audience. Crying babies, unfortunately produced such a wail that many of the items could not be heard.

18 February 1987:   Chess v Woodnewton Junior. Hawthorn won to become Kettering Area Team Champions.

18 November 1987:   Class 2 (Mrs. L. Walker-Hall) visited London. Trip included visit to Planetarium and Science Museum.

18 December 1987:   Mrs. Margaret Watson retired after some seventeen years at this school.

10 March 1988:   A party of 70 children and 4 staff visited the Apollo Theatre, Oxford to see a programme of "The Mister Men and the Space Pirates".

30 June 1988:   Classes 6 and 7 visited Twycross Zoo.

13 July 1988:   Social evening attended by all staff to say "goodbye" to Mr. Bob Scotney (35 years service at this school) and Mrs. Helen Jones (3½ years). Mr. Scotney's service encompassed 3 Head Teachers and countless children. A very loyal associate of this school. Mrs. Jones has been appointed as Deputy Head at Burton Latimer Meadowside Infant School.

1 July 1989:   Craft Fayre held at school. A murky, but not wet day, 15 craft stalls, bouncy castle, swimming pool, childrens games, barbecue and bar, childrens country dancing and 3 folk dancing groups. A very enjoyable and successful day - £450 raised.

13 December 1989:   A Christmas Music Concert was held in the evening. This involved the Junior Choir, the Infant Choir and the Drama Group. A splendid evening.

<u>17 February 1990:</u>	A very successful Barn Dance was held at the school. All of the available 110 tickets were sold (and many more could have been sold had space permitted).
<u>2,3,4 April 1990:</u>	Junior Concert, "Pimlico Drudge" presented to school and parents. An excellent performance.
<u>4-8 June 1990:</u>	Residential school visit to Sandown I.O.W. 27 children, accompanied by Mr. R. Hall, Mrs. L. Walker-Hall and Mrs. P. Deane-Hall (ancillary).
<u>9 January 1991:</u>	Party of 120 children visited Derngate to see "Snow White".
<u>Summer 1991:</u>	A sum of c. £650 had been donated to the school to purchase an extra nimbus computer, with the compliments of the Parents Association.
<u>26 February 1992:</u>	Mrs. Jane Watson and the Headteacher attended training session for managing local bank account.
<u>Summer Term 1992:</u>	Successful residential visit to Scarborough. 28 children supervised by Mr. Coleman, Mrs. Halliday and Miss Rose.
<u>7-11 June 1993:</u>	31 children accompanied by Mrs. J. Evans, Mrs. J. Watson and Mr. I. Peden visited Weymouth. This residential visit had been a great success.
<u>Summer 1997:</u>	School recently enjoyed a visit from "Caliche", two South American musicians who entertained everyone with wonderful music and involved the children in workshop opportunities.
<u>Summer 1997:</u>	Hawthorn won the Kettering Schools Girls Swimming Trophy. The photograph shows the Champion team of Marcia Eaton,

68

Sophie Watts, Cassida Lynch and Hayley Curchin with teacher Mrs. Clubley.

-- oOo --   -- oOo --   -- oOo --

Chapter Seven

The School Centenary

Memories of 100 years ago

THE copy of the letter from Head Teacher Richard Hall that follows contains the inaugural information regarding the School Centenary celebrations. It was distributed during November 1992, giving parents, friends, pupils, governors and staff plenty of notice regarding a 100th birthday celebration which was not theoretically due until 1 May 1995. Work upon the building of the school however had commenced during 1894.

-- oOo --

The Hawthorn Collection

Thoughts of 1894

Hawthorn County Primary School

Dear Parents,

Hawthorn School will be 100 years old in 1994.

This milestone in the history of our school cannot pass by without due recognition.

At school we have already had initial discussions about the possible calendar for our celebratory year beginning in September 1993. This letter is intended to report on some preliminary plans and to encourage response and participation from a wider audience other than those who are part of Hawthorn School today.

Sadly the school log books dating back to the period before 1971 are lost. They would serve as an invaluable encyclopedia of knowledge about life at Hawthorn since 1894.

The oldest document in the school is a punishment book dating back to the 1930's. Caning children at that time was a feature of school life and some names occur quite frequently.

The school also possesses school photographs and scrap books from about 1960.

Other than these artifacts we possess little else save our own memories of Hawthorn over the last decade or so.

It is anticipated that our celebrations will feature three main strands:-

1)   EVENTS
To involve pupils, past and present; parents, teachers and the wider community.

These may take many forms and might include:

(a)   Re-unions

72

(b)	Exhibitions
(c)	Victorian Music Hall
(d)	Victorian Days
(e)	Seasonal Events

Naturally it is hoped that our current pupils will gain much from these events.

The hundred years since the opening of Hawthorn have been, to say the very least, eventful and our celebrations will encourage us to focus upon events and the changing world during this period.

2)   A BOOK OF NOSTALGIA

There must be so many memories of school life at Hawthorn. The Centenary celebration gives us the ideal opportunity to collate a selection. Contributions will be sought from those who have had previous contact with our school as pupils, parents, teachers and others. The final published document should be a fascinating "sampler" of Hawthorn School.

3)   A BUILDING EXTENSION

This final idea is much the most ambitious objective of our centenary. The physical shape of our school has changed little over the last century even though the interior has (somehow) kept pace with current trends. Each entrance to the school passes by a toilet which does little to endear the school to visitors. The school, however, is much more than its entrances and has a character well worth preserving. The facilities at the school though can be improved without fundamentally changing the interior building.

Providing enough finance can be realized it is intended to develop a reception unit at the side of the school utilizing the present Class 1 (Mr. Peden's room) and Class 8 (Mrs. Ashby's room). This reception unit will be in the form of an extension giving extra space and affording better toilet facilities for reception age children and boys. The current boys cloak area and toilet will then be developed to provide an enhanced office/reception area and a medical room (much required in this school).

At this stage we are anxious to prepare a register of former pupils, ex-parents and ex-members of staff who wish to be kept informed of events. You are therefore invited to complete and return the attached form.

You need not add your own name to this list.

Finally can I invite any parent to contact the school if they have ideas for appropriate centenary events and/or schemes for fund raising.

Yours sincerely,

R.A. HALL
HEAD TEACHER

-- oOo ---

THE following sixteen pages represent the "School Centenary Pack", which was sent to parents of pupils of the school in 1993, to former pupils and teachers who had made contact with the school and also to families having a connection with the school at that time.

Unfortunately the school could not supply me with a copy which I badly required for research for this book, but following an appeal within the columns of the Herald and Post during June 2007, <u>one copy of the pack</u> came to light. Graham Jones, from the Pytchley Road area of Kettering, phoned to offer his copy on loan, a copy that he had carefully retained for fourteen years. Thank you Graham, I am most grateful to you!

As the Centenary booklet, for reasons unknown as yet to me, appeared to fall by the wayside, I wondered how many of the proposed Centenary events had been successful. I resolved to have a chat, if possible, with Mrs. Judy Barney who is still teaching at Hawthorn as I write, in the hope that she may be willing and able to shed light in my darkness!

-- oOo --

Hawthorn Primary
1894-1994

Hawthorn County Primary School

Hawthorn Road
Kettering
Northants NN15 7HT

Telephone
(0536) 512204

Headteacher
Richard Hall
BA, Dip Ed.

Mr G Jones
Kettering
Northants
NN15

October 1993

Dear Mr Jones

Thank you for requesting information about our forthcoming school Centenary. I have pleasure in enclosing our School Centenary Pack together with further details about some forthcoming events and fund raising schemes.

We have attempted to contact as many former pupils as possible and have been very pleased with the interest thus far shown. A school as old as ours has a rich history and has touched the lives of many. Contact with former pupils reassures us that much affection exists for our old building and very many fond memories remain of schooldays at Hawthorn. It is fitting therefore that our plans for the year should enable as many as possible to become involved throughout the year.

It is with regret that we cannot trace our school log books back to earlier than 1971 for they would truly have been an invaluable historical source. Despite this problem we are hoping to build up and document a picture of school life since 1894. You will see from the enclosed that plans for the original part of Hawthorn School were drawn up by Gotch & Saunders and the foundation stone high up on the front wall is dated 1894. Just when the school first opened is, at present unknown but we can see that the building was somewhat smaller than it now is. It seems logical and reasonable that we should add 100 to 1894 and begin to plan our birthday celebrations.

During the year we are planning three major events for our centenary. These are:

77

1) A programme of events for pupils, past and present, and friends of the school (Appendix A).

2) A Centenary booklet to celebrate the ten decades of Hawthorn school life (Appendix B).

3) A building programme planned to enhance the main building little changed since 1905 (Appendix C).

Information about each of these is given on attached sheets within the pack.

Our plan to build an extension to the school is much the most ambitious project. A Centenary Steering Group consisting of members of the Governing Body, the teaching staff and the Parents' Association have had meetings to discuss this project. Any building work necessarily requires money and a fund raising schedule has been established. Some of the events/activities are to be organised by the Parents' Association as part of their efforts to raise money towards the building, others by the school.

However not all of our thoughts should be centred upon fund raising and we hope that you will enjoy the opportunity to be involved without serious damage to your pocket!

It is not too late to send in your anecdotes and memories of your days at school, either as parent or child. Last term a number of former pupils were interviewed and their recollections fascinated our present day pupils.

Today at school we have children whose brothers, sisters, parents, uncles, aunts and grandparents all attended Hawthorn. This family connection helps give our school the unique character that it enjoys.

This history and our own attachment to the present school building and community encourages us to make the most of our birthday. Our present day pupils and their families will all be fully involved and it is to be hoped that those of you to whom we now write will both support and welcome our correspondence and planned activities.

During the coming months we will be writing regular news letters to you. Look out for our mascot Pip Berry who is set firm to invade your life.

We look forward to your continuing interest and support.

Yours sincerely,

Richard Hall
Headteacher

-- oOo --   -- oOo --

APPENDIX A

Programme of Centenary Events

Further information about all of these events will be sent out during the year.

Centenary Launch	- Wednesday 22 September 1993
Bumper Christmas Fayre	- Friday 26 November 1993
Magic Lantern Show	- Spring 1994
Promises Evening	- Spring 1994
Victorian Photographs	- Spring 1994
Flower Festival	- Spring 1994
Victorian May Day	- May 1994
Display of Work	- June/July 1994
Summer Fayre (pig roast?)	- June 1994
School Picnic	- June 1994
Palace of Variety	- July 1994
Street Party	- September 1994
Victorian Music Evening	- December 1994
1970-1980)	- Friday 15 October 1993
Reunions 1960-1970)	- Friday 25 February 1994
Pre 1960)	- Friday 10 June 1994
School Visits for former pupils	- See attached list

Our present school Parents' Association is also planning a programme of events which are aimed to complement the above list. Information about these events will also be circulated.

During the school year our present pupils will learn much about life since 1894. The display of work will no doubt reflect the changing pattern of society during these last 100 years.

APPENDIX B

As part of our celebrations we are going to compile a book of memories and stories, drawings and photographs, poems and anecdotes by pupils and teachers, past and present.

We invite you to contribute to this book which we hope will reflect the ten decades of school life. If you are able to "put pen to paper" we would hope to receive your item by 16 July 1993. Please make sure that you include your name, your status (pupil, parent, teacher etc.) and your period of school involvement.

For those of you who live locally we would like some of our present pupils to record an interview with you. Perhaps if you live away from Kettering it may be possible for you to visit the school to be interviewed "on site". Your memories will be of great interest to our present pupils and must surely be a rich source of material for our Centenary book.

When compiled, and the school reserves editorial rights, the book will be printed, bound and made available for purchase.

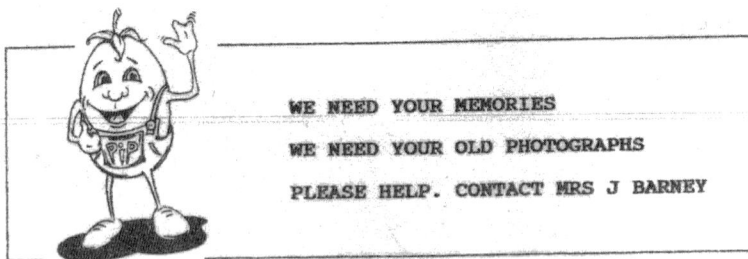

WE NEED YOUR MEMORIES

WE NEED YOUR OLD PHOTOGRAPHS

PLEASE HELP. CONTACT MRS J BARNEY

Another idea being considered is the compilation of a Centenary Cook Book to include recipes new and old. Perhaps you have ideas that you wish to share with us. Mrs. Maureen Buckerfield has volunteered to assist us with this venture and she may be contacted through the school.

If you are able to contribute an article for our Centenary Book, offer a recipe for our 100 year cook book or make yourself available for an interview, we invite you to complete the attached slip and return it to school.

Thank you for your help

APPENDIX C

Centenary Building Scheme

The existing structure of Hawthorn School has changed little since 1905 and the entrances through which the pupils entered the school are still in use.

Since the provision of inside toilets (perhaps you may remember the age of outside loos?) entrance to the school now requires a side step past a toilet block, a feature which is uniquely Hawthorn but hardly complimentary to our fine school.

We have ambitions therefore to build an extension which will afford a new entrance. Within this new entrance will be a reception area/secretary's office attached to which will be a medical room (a resource so badly needed at school). This extension will also enable us to improve classroom provision.

Additional to this is a desire to build a room which will further serve the local community. At present our very successful Playschool attends to the needs of many pre-school children and two thriving Mums and Tots groups meet on the school premises. A new community amenity built on the school premises would consolidate this provision and allow the possibility of another, older, generation of users to make use of our school.

All of this of course requires money and lots of it! Approaches have been made to the County Council but to no avail. Recent changes have meant a shrinking allocation of money available for capital expenditure in schools and therefore a rigid prioritising of how the money is spent. We might argue that our need is great but it is difficult to argue that it is greater than many others.

We therefore hope to raise sufficient funds ourselves to enable this building programme to go ahead. This will no doubt involve applications to various charitable foundations, fund raising activities and direct contributions. Many ideas have already been discussed and, once again, we hope to receive your support. We realize that our current parent community cannot be expected to raise the sum of money which will be involved so we appeal to those of you who now live further afield to help us in any way you can.

At the moment plans are being developed and costed out and as soon as these are available you will receive all relevant information.

-- *oOo* --

PROMISES EVENING (March 1994)

The Parents Association are planning to organise a Promises Evening at which the audience are invited to bid for gifts, services etc. provided by the supporters.

We hope that this event will prove to be a bumper success following as it does a very enjoyable first attempt which was held in the Autumn of last year.

Perhaps you can donate something for our Promises Evening. A future news letter will request donations.

SCHOOL VISITS FOR FORMER PUPILS

These will take place at the following times:

The number of visitors will be limited to 20 on any one visit. Please note that certain visits have been designated for attendance years.

1.	1970 – 1980	Monday 11 October 1993	1.30 – 3.30
2.	Open	Monday 22 November 1993	1.30 – 3.30
3.	Pre 1960	Wednesday 2 February 1994	1.30 – 3.30
4.	Open	Tuesday 8 March 1994	1.30 – 3.30
5.	1960 – 1970	Tuesday 26 April 1994	1.30 – 3.30
6.	Open	Wednesday 6 June 1994	1.30 – 3.30

SCHOOL VISITS FOR FORMER PUPILS

Please complete

Full name . . . .

Address . . . .

. . . .

. . . .

Telephone number . . . .

84

Preferred visit day in order of preference

(1)   (2)   (3)

Places will be allocated upon receipt of request.

The school will write to confirm your visit two weeks before the scheduled date.

SCHOOL REUNIONS

You are invited to attend our school reunions to help celebrate the School's Centenary Year. The dates are as follows:

1970 – 1980   Friday 15 October 1993

1960 – 1970   Friday 25 February 1994

Pre 1960   Friday 10 June 1994

Tickets are £3.00 per person to include a buffet. To reserve your tickets please complete and return the attached slip.

- -

SCHOOL REUNIONS

Name . . . .

Address . . . .

. . . .

. . . .

Number of tickets required . . . .   1970 – 1980

. . . .   1960 – 1970

. . . .   Pre 1960

85

BUY A BRICK

I am sure that this scheme needs no introduction.

We are inviting former pupils to make a direct donation towards our fund raising efforts.

The planned building extension will cost perhaps £100,000

Our Parents' Association will be hoping to raise £10,000

The school will raise £10,000

The pupils at the school are aiming to raise £500

Our successful Playschool will raise £3,000

We hope that former pupils will help us raise between £5,000 and £10,000

The rest of the money we must gain from Grants and Charitable Trusts.

Can you help?

Our buy a brick scheme asks for a donation of £5 per brick and we hope to "sell" 2,000 bricks.

Names of donors will be recorded in our Brick book where our thanks can be permanently recorded.

Each entry in our Brick book will be:

Name	Association Date
Address	Special Message

See example below:

Mr James Friend	Parent 1957 – 72
2 Weasel Road	
Rugby	'For my sons
Warwickshire	Thankyou!'

You are welcome to buy as many bricks as you wish up to a maximum of 5.

Please complete and return the attached slip together with your contribution and Thank you for your help.

HAWTHORN COUNTY PRIMARY SCHOOL CENTENARY APPEAL

BUY A BRICK SCHEME

I would like to donate .... brick(s) at a cost of £5 each. I enclose the sum of £.........

Please make cheques payable to Hawthorn County Primary School Centenary Fund.

Name ....

Address ....

....

....

-- oOo --

Within this scheme we are hoping to sell a year to either individuals or businesses. A donation of £50 or more will purchase a year (and so a page) in our Centenary Year Book.

Entries in this book may well appear as below:

1926

Geo. Williams and Sons Ltd.
Manufacturers of machine tools

Est. 1936

Mr Mark Williams   pupil 1961 – 1968

Mrs Harriet Williams

Each entry can be individually tailored to meet your needs.

If you wish to reserve an entry in our year book please complete and return the attached application.

CENTENARY YEAR BOOK 1894 – 1994

Full name . . . .

Address . . . .

. . . .

. . . .

Telephone number . . . .

Planned entry:

I enclose a donation of £ ……….. towards your building fund.

I understand that if my year is duplicated with another request then priority will be given in order of receipt.

-- o0o --

You will know, having studied our Centenary Pack, that we have a number of celebration events planned over the forthcoming months. Added to this list are:

1)   A sponsored walk (possible date 17 October 1993).

2)   Bonanza Christmas Fayre 26 November 1993.

3)   Fashion Show "Through the Ages" 10 February 1994

4)   Mid summer Fayre June 1994.

89

Hawthorn County Primary School
Hawthorn Road
Kettering
Northants
NN15 7HT

Telephone (0536) 512204

Teaching Staff

Mr Richard Hall – Headteacher
Mr Mike Coleman – Deputy Head Teacher
Mrs Mary Ashby
Mr Paul Aucott
Mrs Judy Barney
Mrs Paulette Deane Hall
Mrs Linda Dix
Mrs Susan Eden
Mrs Julie Evans
Mrs Mary Halliday
Mr Iain Peden
Miss Sally Rose
Miss Jane Wingrave

Support Staff

Mrs Jane Watson – Secretary/Bursar
Mrs Sarah Tawn – Clerical Assistant
Mrs Penny Fox – Classroom Assistant
Mrs Sarah Smith – Classroom Assistant
Mrs Linda Woodcock – Classroom Assistant
Mrs Lucy Oliver Carton – Resources
Mr David Hurcombe – Site Supervisor
Mrs Nicky Holmes – Grounds Keeper

Dining Room Supervisors

Mrs Pauline Clark
Mrs Jackie Downes
Mrs Maureen Eaton
Mrs Janet Gilbert
Mrs Nicky Holmes
Mrs Kay Murphy
Mrs Gillian Schultze

Please Note

This correspondence is being sent out to:

    (a)   Parents of current pupils.

    (b)   Former pupils / teachers who have made contact with the school.

    (c)   Last known addresses of families having connection with the school.

If you do not wish to receive further information, or if this pack is wrongly addressed, please contact the school and your name and/or address will be removed from our mailing list.

-- oOo --

We will be delighted to receive extra names of former pupils/teachers etc. who have connection with the school. Please contact the school office on Kettering (0536) 512204.

Thank you for your help

Hawthorn Community Primary School
October 1993

-- oOo --

91

I caught up with Judy Barney one school lunchtime and during our chat in the school reception area she revealed that the Centenary Booklet had not been produced and a number of the other suggested functions had to be curtailed. There had just been no-one available who could cope with the extra work and responsibility during what had been an extremely busy period at the school. She supplied me with a little of the background to matters at that time and also kindly gave me a number of names, who if contacted might remember something of the Centenary celebrations.

So, I came to meet up with Mike Coleman (Deputy Head Teacher 1974-2004) who certainly had some memories to share. He also quickly confirmed Judy Barney's story that for various reasons all of the events could not take place, as there were after all approximately two dozen mentioned within the Centenary Pack and the staff at that time were already dreadfully stretched. However, almost without exception, those events that were put on went extremely well and were really enjoyed by both participants and audiences.

-- oOo --

The Centenary Committee decided that a logo would help in promoting their Appeal Fund and following consultations with the children, "Pip Berry" was decided upon, being derived from the Hawthorn Berries Playgroup logo.

"Pip" was presented on memorabilia that was offered for sale to children and parents – white china mugs were most popular, indeed perhaps surprisingly several were still to be found and were proudly displayed, even as I researched this book. "Pip" also appeared on 'T' shirts, yellow and green plastic Hawthorn mugs and also on pens and pencils. In fact his was rather a well known figure around the southern side of Kettering and he certainly did his share in promoting the Centenary cause!

-- oOo --

The Centenary launch was planned for Wednesday 22 September 1993 and took place in the school hall. It was very well attended by pupils and parents, the highlight being two mock classrooms which had been set up in the hall, one being of current schooling systems, with calculators and computers, the other being a "Mike Coleman" version of a Victorian school room with appropriate "props" and dress code! The latter was more appreciated by the visitors who in truth couldn't really know how right or wrong Mike was with his interpretation of school in the 1890's, but they certainly enjoyed his ideas and costume and perhaps not unnaturally his class was far noisier than the 1993 version.

-- oOo --

A fashion show was staged in the hall during February 1994 with the theme "Fashion Through the Ages".

-- oOo --

The Summer Fayre went ahead and indeed created a worthy profit, but the "pig roast" was eventually considered possibly too ambitious, so a barbecue with sausages and burgers was substituted without too much complaint from the clients.

-- oOo --

Photographs of the children were taken in their Victorian costumes and were presented with sepia surrounds to give a little Victorian authenticity.

-- oOo --

The reunions for past pupils went off very well from October 1993, until June 1994. All being extremely well attended. It has been said, however that possibly the one glass of wine per head which was on offer, contributed to a distinctly convivial atmosphere!

-- oOo --

The "Buy a Brick" scheme created interest as parents paid their £5.00 per brick to leave their name and message recorded in the Brick Book and the Centenary Appeal Fund was suitably swollen by the donations thus collected.

-- oOo --

The school Victorian picnic was arranged for 5 July 1994 in Wicksteed Park. The children left school around 11.30 a.m. suitably dressed in their Victorian garb, accompanied by available parents. Following arrival at the Park, lunch was taken in class and family groups. Afterwards live entertainment was provided by fire eaters, a clown and Punch and Judy, followed by games and races. However, the highlight of the day was the train ride around the Park which everyone really enjoyed and which brought a lovely day out to a very happy conclusion.

-- oOo --

The Victorian Music Hall, termed a "Centenary of Celebration" was a great success, held at the McKinlay Theatre during July 1994. The Show included a number of guest supporters of the Centenary appeal, The Irthlingborough Entertainment Society, The Innovations Musical Theatre Company and Rushden Operatic, to name but three groups that provided memories from eras between 1890 and 1990. Amongst favourite excerpts were snapshots from Joseph, Annie, Bootleg Beatles and Disney from the pupils and their guests. *"it was a great evening"*, remembered Mike Coleman, *"the children performed brilliantly and really enjoyed themselves!"*

Hawthorn County Primary School

A Century of Celebration

PROGRAMME

ACT I

OLIVER 1890
Hawthorn School

GILBERT & SULLIVAN 1900
The Savoyards - Julie Evans and Clifford Allan

BUGSY MALONE 1920
Hawthorn School

TAP DANCING 1920's
Katy Watson and Robert Blaxley

GERSHWIN 1930's
Rushden Operatic Society

ANNIE 1930/40
Hawthorn School

ACT II

ROCK & ROLL YEARS
Innovations Musical Theatre Co

BOOTLEG BEATLES 1960
Hawthorn School

PIANO MAGIC
Louisa Lam and Francis Lam

DISNEY MAGIC 1970
Hawthorn School

BARNUM 1980/90
Irthlingborough Entertainment Society

JOSEPH 1990
Hawthorn School

1894 - 1994

D.L. Photography

94

The Street Party was planned to perfection. Hawthorn Road was closed off at both the Argyle Street and Garfield Street ends. Sadly, however the weather had not been planned properly, as it proved to be cold and damp. Undeterred the children, attired in a magnificent variety of fancy dress costumes, paraded along the street and back again into the school for the "Street Party".

Maureen Eaton Collection

Mike did say that a huge banner was hung across the street, right over the road, proclaiming the day – and sure enough Maureen Eaton kindly provided a photograph, taken by her late husband Roger, which proved that Mike's memory is not yet failing him!

-- oOo --

The Flower Festival took place at the Toller Church. Pupils, parents, teachers and the PTA joined together to create "A Themed Flower Display". Mike Coleman remembers some really marvellous exhibits. "*Most professional and artistic*", he commented.

Hawthorn County Primary School

FLOWER FESTIVAL

Welcome to our Festival

This event is being staged as part of the schools' Centenary Celebrations. All proceeds from this event will be in aid of our School Building Fund We hope you enjoy our arrangements.

Thankyou for your support

Richard Hall. Headteacher.

D.L. Photography

The display was open to the public and a silver collection was sought from viewers.

-- oOo --

Hawthorn School has a teacher of some rarity on the staff at present, as Linda Dix is a Morris Dancer. In fact she is more than that, she is a Morris Dance Teacher. She also sings folk songs, plays the guitar, the melodian and the concertina. She has been at Hawthorn since 1986 and plans all the school dances and dance related functions. She was wholly responsible for the 1995 Centenary May Day dance planning, which involved the whole school, from 9.15 a.m. until late afternoon on that fine May Monday. All pupils took part at some time during the day, from the Playschool children to the Senior Juniors, with a grand finale of "The Lord of the Dance", which was received extremely well by the gathered parents and friends.

The Hawthorn Collection

As is the Hawthorn custom the Centenary May Queen and King, (Jade Gardner and Stevie Robey) were duly crowned by the retiring Queen and King, at the commencement of the festivities.

-- oOo --

Following my meeting with Mike Coleman I called upon Maureen Buckerfield who, in addition to being a pupil at Hawthorn (1952-1958), spent a number of years as a "Hawthorn Helper". Being at a Centenary Appeal meeting one day she suggested that the

96

Centenary Cook Book could be a potential money spinner. Of course in the way that matters develop, she was elected as "Cook Book Co-ordinator". The appeal for 100 recipes was remarkably successful and amazingly Maureen tried and tested each one herself. Then she presented her manuscript to Mrs. Jane Watson, the then School Secretary who was responsible for the typing, duplicating and binding. Although sadly Maureen's memory has been fogged by time, regarding how many cook books were sold, she does remember that the book was a great success and was financially yet another, "brick in the wall", so to speak, of the school extension!!

Her final words to me, as I took my leave of her were, *"If you only try but just one recipe, make it the pineapple fruit cake, it is so delicious!!"*

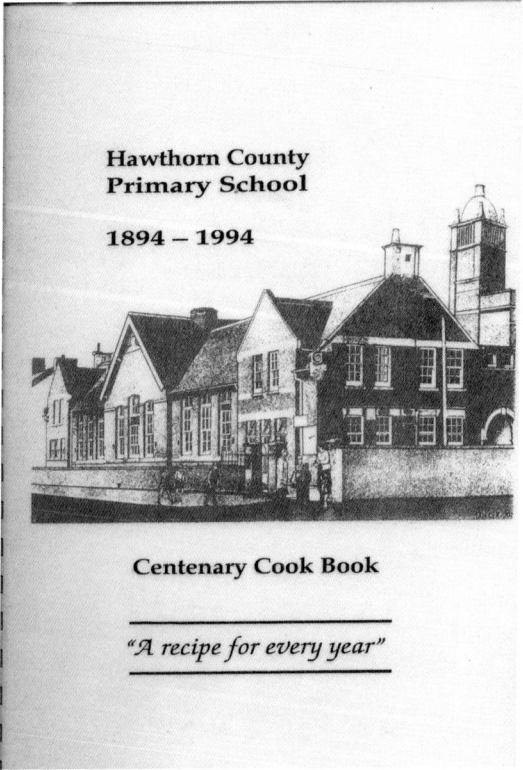

Hawthorn County Primary School

1894 – 1994

Centenary Cook Book

"A recipe for every year"

D.L. Photography

I did and it was!

Pineapple Fruit Cake Recipe

12oz mixed fruit
4oz chopped glace cherries
Small tin crushed pineapple
2 eggs

6oz soft brown sugar
4oz margarine
8oz S.R. flour

Method:
Boil together fruit, cherries, sugar, margarine and crushed pineapple. Allow to cool.
When cold add flour and eggs.
Use an 8 inch greased tin. Bake mixture at Gas Mark 2, 300° for 1¾ hours.

- A deliciously moist fruit cake -

-- oOo --

A number of other functions were held under the Centenary label, some of course more popular than others.

During March 1994 a large Craft Fair pulled in the crowds and a Race Night the following month, organised by the PTA in the Kettering General Hospital Social Club, created lots of interest for many who had never previously experienced such an evening. On 2 July 1994, "Pips Summer Camp" took the form of a School Summer Fayre which made a good financial return for the cause. One of the final functions organised was a PTA Barn Dance at the Corn Market Hall during May 1995. To conclude the celebrations a Centenary Dinner and Ball took place at the Wicksteed Park Pavilion.

It was obvious that maximum effort had been put into the Centenary celebrations by all interested parties – the Headteacher and staff, the Governors, the parents, the PTA, various friends of the School, and of course the children.

The whole exercise was most worthwhile as sometime later the fine building extension was opened with due ceremony by Phil Sawford, the local M.P. It had proved a tough journey, but the final result was seen to be well worth the sometime bumpy ride!

-- oOo --

98

The following memories are taken from the letters received by the school from ex-pupils and staff around the time of the school Centenary Celebrations. Most were in response to the Centenary Pack which was sent out to certain ex-pupils during mid-October 1993. Some letters however are a result of press publicity or even by word of mouth via friends, relatives or colleagues. I want to thank Richard Hall for kindly allowing me access to this material and I hope that contributors have no problem with my reproducing their correspondence within this Hawthorn book. Sadly however a number of these contributors have now passed away.

-- oOo --

From K. WINSTONE OF WINDSOR GARDENS, KETTERING
My mother was born in 1896 and she started at Hawthorn when she was 3 or 4 (1899/1900). The Headmistress was Miss Clarke and because of her dumpy appearance was known as "Fatty" Clarke

Classmates that mother remembered were the Holden children, and a girl named Nicholls.

-- oOo --

From MAY WILSON of MALVERN, WORCESTERSHIRE (1908-1914)
I started at Hawthorn in 1908, just before my fifth birthday. The children were learning their letters, some having large cardboard ones worn around their necks. As I could read I went into the second class where we used slates and we were not supposed to let our slate pencils squeak.

Mr. Cartwright was Headmaster in the big school and classes were 50 to 60 but well behaved. For talking out of turn in class we had to put our hands on our head and stand out in the front.

The teacher who we thought a "dragon" was Miss Cox the needlework teacher. We had a small square of white cotton material to hem, then gather and set into a band. Then we made a buttonhole. If our stitches were not small and even, they had to be unpicked and re-done. I was

99

never very good at sewing and my work got dirtier and spotted with blood from pricked fingers.

I left in 1914 having passed the County Scholarship to Kettering High School in Bowling Green Road.

My brother started at Hawthorn in 1903 and my sister in 1904. Our name was Abraham and we lived in Garfield Street.

May Wilson visited the school on Tuesday 21 September 1993, when she was 90 years of age.

-- oOo --

From MISS OLGA PACHESA, POLWELL LANE, BARTON SEAGRAVE

I am the step-daughter of Ernest Walker Ward born at Pytchley. He died 5 October 1960, aged 71.

He was a teacher as a young man. In fact I think Hawthorn Road School was his first real post after training. There were no buses then so his journey to school from Pytchley was through the fields and during winter, through deep snow as well.

-- oOo --

From V.R. FOSTER, BOWHILL – KETTERING (1914-1920)

I started at the Infants School in September 1914. I was taught by Miss Anstey and Miss Jones. Both of them were very nice ladies who were loved by all children.

On moving on to the infants higher classes we were first taught by Miss Ketcher and then by Miss Cook. These two were greatly disliked by all the children. Miss Cook had a nasty habit of smacking our faces or hitting us across our knuckles with a wooden pointer.

Soon after World War I ended, my teacher was Mr. Penny. He was a great favourite. During the war he had been a soldier, serving at the Indian Army Staff College in

100

Bangalore, never a day passed without him telling us something about India and we were all enthralled by what we heard. He even taught us to recite Gunga Din!

During the war an aeroplane crash landed where Highfield Road is now situated and all the school pupils were taken to see it.

I am enclosing copies of certificates which were given to me in 1916 for taking money to school for the fighting mens comfort.

During my school days a large Union flag hung behind the Headmasters desk in the hall. It bore an inscription that it had been presented by the children of Kettering, Jamaica (It would appear to be Kettering, Tasmania, C.H.)

-- oOo --

From NORA CHEATLE (1923-1929)
1923-24
The reception class was in the large middle room facing on to Hawthorn Road. Here we had cowrie shells in tins for counting and coloured chalks to draw on individual blackboards. We also had sand trays in which we practiced our letters. Friday afternoon was games time. Besides the usual boxes of bricks and board games, there was a large rocking horse in the middle of the floor and a swing suspended in the doorway. The teacher was Miss Watson, a young teacher from Lancashire.

1924-25
In the next class we had cardboard number wheels for addition and subtraction and a "pretend" shop with empty tins and cartons. The teacher was Miss Anstey, a lady with a large bosom and a booming voice – rather intimidating to 6 year olds!

1925-26
The top infant class was known as Standard 1 (possibly a mixed age group). Here we did our first "compositions" with help from words on cards. The girls were taught how to do tacking stitches and running stitches. We also learnt

multiplication tables 1-6. The teacher was Mrs. Woodey who was very strict.

1926-27

Standard 2 was in the classroom at the rostrum end of the west side of the hall. Here we thoroughly learnt tables 7-12, being frequently tested. The class reader was Water Babies which I did not like. The teacher was Miss Huckbody who left in the next year to train to be a missionary in India.

1927-28

I was promoted to Standard 4 in the room with windows to the back playground. There was a choice of library books which included "Round the world in eighty days", "Arabian Nights" and "Rip van Winkle". The teacher was Miss Ethel Kingsbury (now Mrs. E. Corby) who introduced us to Shakespeare! I greatly enjoyed what must have been children's versions of "As You Like It" and "The Merchant of Venice".

1928-29

Standard 5 was the scholarship class. There were between 45 and 50 children but we learnt a lot. There were weekly tests in reading, writing, spelling and mental arithmetic. The class reader was Ivanhoe which I did not like. (Obviously an introduction to Scott at the age of 10 is off-putting!). We coloured rainfall maps and contour maps and learned the capitals of all the countries in the world. There was also a most interesting date chart at picture rail level along two of the walls: from the Romans to the Normans on one and 1066 to present day on the other. The teacher was Mr. Roland Ginns who capably coped with what must have been a difficult situation.

As this was before re-organisation, there were 12-14 year olds in the school i.e. those who did not pass to go to the High School, the Grammar School or the Central School. These were in the classroom in the far corner of the hall with Mr. Ernest Ward as teacher. Girls were taught cookery in the room upstairs and the boys were taken to the woodwork centre in School Lane.

Standard 5 joined with Standards 6 and 7 for singing under the conductorship of Mr. Ward. The songs I remember are "The Keeper", "Strawberry Fair" and "Dashing away with the smoothing iron" and my favourite was Rubenstein's "Melody in F" with the words "Through the green woodland when morning is bright".

Mr. Edgar Markham was the Headmaster and he led morning assemblies in the hall. Here we learnt and recited Bible passages: Psalms 23, 24, 121 and 103.

They were very happy days and a sound foundation was laid for further education wherever that was to be.

-- oOo --

From MRS. MARGARET BARWELL (nee BELL), IPSWICH, SUFFOLK (1925-1931)

As an old pupil I heard with great interest of next years 100th Reunion. I attended 1925-1931 under Mr. Markham, with wonderful teachers especially Miss Kingsbury (later Mrs. Corby) and Mr. Moule. My school days were the happiest days of my life and I cried when I had to leave.

-- oOo --

From ROY KING, CHURCH ROAD, PYTCHLEY (1927-1933)

I started at Hawthorn Road during 1927 as a five year old. Our Headmaster was Mr. Markham, who retired after I had been a pupil for two years. (Edgar Markham was quite ill for some time before he finally retired during April 1931 – C.H.) He was followed by Mr. Hudson, who was a retired Captain from the Army. My first infant school teacher was Miss Anstey, a very sweet lady. I call to mind the big rocking horse that used to stand in the infant corridor, and the many rides we used to have.

Miss Butler was another teacher I remember. She used to play the piano as each class marched to its own classroom each morning and afternoon. Almost every playtime throughout the summer months Mr. Hudson and Mr. Moule, the only other male teacher, used to play cricket with us. We used a large metal waste paper basket as the wickets, wire frames were made to fit over the windows, to *keep the breakages down! In the winter we played football, half the school played up hill (the uppers), the other played downhill (the downers). I remember Mr. Launden, the Caretaker. He used to return to school in winter about 9.00 p.m. each evening in order to stoke the boiler so that we might keep <u>almost</u> warm enough the next day, to write without shaking too much. However if we got too cold we used to put on our overcoats and run around the playground, then back to our classroom, all nice and warm.*

Just a few happy thoughts of days at Hawthorn Road School.

-- oOo --

From MAMIE HOOPER (nee WESTLEY) (1929-1935)
In 1929 when I was five, I became a pupil in the infants class at Hawthorn Road. The very same day Eva Whitwell joined the class. She became my greatest friend and remains so to this very day. We were in every class together and went on to the High School and have shared our lives ever since.

I remember "Captain" Hudson as he liked to be called. His greatest pleasure was to teach us good handwriting. "Up thin, down thick", we used to chant as we wrote with our dipping pens from our ink wells. How we all tried to copy his perfect handwriting! He would walk up and down the rows of desks with a ruler in his hands, ready to give us a reminder if we were not working well enough!

Work hard boys and girls of Hawthorn Road, value your school and above all, value the friendships you will make and may they last a lifetime.

-- oOo --

From BARBARA TAYLOR (nee BELL) (1930-1937)
I still have two books that were presented as prizes to me whilst at school.

One of these books was presented after a visit to the Kaycee Clothing factory in Dryden Street, for an essay I

104

produced about this visit. Kettering Co-operative Society used to present a scholarship each year for either the High School or the Grammar School, to the person who gained the highest marks in an exam about the Co-operative Movement, in conjunction with the marks gained in the County Scholarship examination. Several of the pupils from Hawthorn entered for the Co-operative Scholarship and the visit to the Kaycee factory was in preparation for this exam.

I was happily awarded the Co-op Scholarship and also a County Scholarship. As the latter included a school uniform grant, in addition to paying Kettering High School fees, I gratefully accepted it. The Co-operative Scholarship was then awarded to Pat Curtis also from Hawthorn, who I remember used to live in Hawthorn Road.

Both my sister Norah (1924-1931) and brother Colin (1933-1940) attended Hawthorn!

-- oOo --

From PETER HANGER (1932-1938)

A few days after my fifth birthday I began my school life at Hawthorn Road Infants School. I think it was January 1932 and I started in Miss Jarvis' baby class. She told us fairy stories and encouraged us to go to sleep on some afternoons. During September 1932 we "went up" into Miss Dixon's class and learned addition with coloured counters. A year later we moved up into Miss Anstey's class and were taught sums with shillings and pence. Then I moved into the "big" school and teacher Miss Woodey taught the class (including me) how to knit and I made a needle case for my mother. Nearing the end of my time at Hawthorn I discovered that the school had quite a successful soccer team. I think it was 1937 when in an exciting game against St. Marys School, Hawthorn won 3-2 at the Avondale Playing Fields to win the Taylor Cup. Terry Wright scored a marvellous goal!

-- oOo --

105

<u>From IRIS MAYCOCK (nee DORR), GREENFIELD AVENUE, KETTERING (1935-1941)</u>

I attended Hawthorn from 1935 until moving on to the High School. My children also attended, Nigel from 1961 and Louise from 1966.

My earliest memory is of at the age of 6 years, walking on a plank over the brook between Netherfield Road and Springfield Road, as the road had not been culverted at this time. Captain Hudson was Headmaster then, until he went into the Army, when he was succeeded by Mr. Moule until the war ended.

Before air raid shelters were built at the school, all pupils who lived a fair distance were allocated nearer houses to run to, in the event of an air raid during school hours. I think we only did this once!

-- oOo --

<u>From CHRISTINE MARY RIDLEY (nee LYLES) of NEWCASTLE-UPON-TYNE (C. 1935)</u>

I was at the school for only three years (not stated when).
I distinctly remember queuing to go in, and yes – those brick toilets at the top of the playground!!!

Under the Headmaster, Mr. Hudson, I remember his son Peter periodically took a class in the temporary absence of a teacher, he being on holiday from his public school.

During the war years my mother and father attended rifle handling classes at the school!

-- oOo --

<u>From TREVOR ASHBY (1937-1943)</u>

I started at Hawthorn Road School at the age of four in 1937 carrying on a family connection as my mother and her family had attended the school from the turn of the century. Of my first days in the school I can remember us having small mats on the floor where we were expected to have a nap in mid-afternoon.

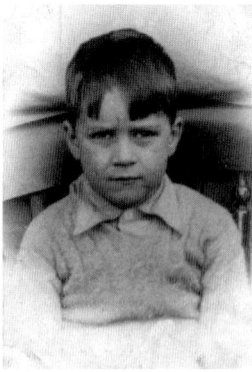

My childhood sweetheart was Esme Bowman but I can't remember what she looked like or where she lived. So much for remembering your first love. My two friends were Geoffrey Neesome who lived in Silverwood Road and Terry Sumpter who lived in that area, but not much else about my school pals remains.

Of the teaching staff the Headmaster was Mr. Moule a small grumpy man who mumbled, or that is how I recall him. Miss Anstey a large kindly woman, Miss Beeby a small lady always on the go and Miss Grudgings strict but fair who was there 'till the 1960's. She was very helpful to my wife when she became a teacher at the school.

A few incidents of school life still remain in my memory. I came shopping to Theobalds with my mother at what I thought was still the school holidays only to see the children in the school playground. When we enquired we found that school had started that morning, and Miss Anstey had a page of sums for me. I was and still am the worlds worst speller, I always had trouble with "which and witch", it must have frustrated my teacher as she sent me to the top infants class to ask them how to spell "which". It's now one of the few words I never spell wrong. I can still hear Miss Beeby's class reciting their three times tables through and then through again in reverse.

During the war a shelter was built in the playground but the children who lived near the school were to be sent home when the siren went. We had a practice drill, I had been briefed by my mother to wait and bring my sister home, which I did, but it took me so long to get home, by the time I got back to school the class were half way through the next lesson.

My last memories of school life relate to when the top class was moved to a church hall in The Grove, Miss Grudgings was the teacher. We were rehearsing a play about a shooting party out of "Pickwick Papers". I can't remember which character I was but I know I was relieved when I left before the public performance!

-- oOo --

From MRS DAPHNE MARCH (nee PAMPLIN), AMBLECOTE, STOURBRIDGE (1937-1939)
I was very interested to read of the schools 100th birthday – the cutting from the Evening Telegraph passed on to me by an old friend Mary Franklin (nee Chapman) who used to live in Hawthorn Road, and attended the school as I did some 56 years ago. My teacher was Miss Butler who was quite wonderful.

I am now aged 64, Mary being a few months younger – we still correspond and consider each other as best friends after all these years.

One of my most vivid memories being that at the outset of World War II, we were to be sent home in the event of an air raid. As I lived by Wicksteed Park it was considered too far for me to travel, so I was to go with Mary to her Hawthorn Road home. We had many a giggle sitting under her stairs during an air raid practice!!

-- oOo --

From MARGARET HOME (nee HUMPHREYS), BOWLING GREEN ROAD, KETTERING (1940'S-1950'S)
It was the 1920's and a widow of a soldier killed in World War I, Mrs. Ada Cooke, my grandmother, lived in Gladstone Street with her three children Betty, Randolph and Philip. All three children went to Hawthorn and although Randolph died when he was twenty one, Betty my mother, and Philip my uncle have some happy memories of the school. The Headmaster at the time was Mr. Markham, which is a very apt name for a Headmaster!

108

He and most of the teachers at the school at that time cycled to school from the outlying villages and other parts of the town as there were hardly any cars about at all in those days.

At that time Hawthorn was not just a primary school, as the pupils stayed on until they were fourteen, at which age they started work.

Philip especially remembers the science lab, as he and his friends used to make blow pipes out of glass tubes. They would use them to blow the yolks out of birds eggs which they collected.

Betty has three particular memories. When she was about 5, her mother had a very pretty dress made for her. Because she looked so lovely in it, she was chosen to take the collection following the school play!

There were no school dinners at that time and all three children had to go home to Gladstone Street and back every lunchtime. One day Betty failed to arrive. Her frantic mother went to the school hoping to find her, but the teachers didn't know where she was either. It so happened that her and a friend had gone into the cattle market in London Road and had climbed into a truck to watch the auctioneer selling the cattle, but afterwards they were too frightened to get out of the truck! They never did get back to school that day!

Another thing Betty remembers is being a fairy in a school play. Her performance was held at the Toller Church Hall in Meeting Lane and it was extremely cold. Mother insisted that she wore a woolly vest. She had no white plimsolls so she borrowed some, two sizes too large! Can you imagine what she looked like in a fairy dress with a large woolly vest underneath and plimsolls far too large for her feet!

Happy memories!

-- oOo --

We attended Hawthorn Road School from 1942 to 1950. At that time part of the infant school was sited in the wooden cricket pavilion in Lewis Road. Two classes were there, taken by Miss Thomas and Mrs. March. The pavilion had a big stove in the middle and in winter the frozen milk was put next to it to thaw. The milk bottle tops were cardboard with a push-out middle to put the straw through. When washed the tops made ideal rings for making woollen pompoms.

Around the walls of the pavilion were pictures showing numbers and letters drawn in pastel crayon by the teachers. We had slates to write on, which were pushed down a slit in the front of the desk when not in use. We used slate pencils which made a terrible noise when dragged across the surface. In the junior school we graduated to 'dip-in' pens with steel nibs and used powdered ink in china ink wells, which made for very messy workbooks!

As we were war babies the Welfare State provided us with orange juice and cod liver oil which we took every morning, drinking from fish paste jars. In addition we had to carry gas masks with us in cardboard boxes (one Donald Duck and one Mickey Mouse).

In the summer the whole of the cricket field was our playground and we used to make daisy chains and play in the mown grass, to the detriment of our clothing, not to mention our legs.

When we were seven we transferred to the junior school in Hawthorn Road. As far as we can remember some of the staff at that time were: Miss Everett (infants), Miss Wright, Miss Macintosh, Miss Cawston, Miss Grudgings, Mr. Payne, Mr. Smith, Mr. Pringle, Mr. Burkill and Mr. Wigley. The headmasters were Mr. Hudson followed by Mr. Bird.

Yes, we remember the outdoor lavatories, especially in 1947, the year of the great snow. We had to cross the playground through a passage cut in the snow, which was higher than our heads. One of the highlights of the winter term was having enough snow for a snowball fight at playtime against the boys, over the playground wall, especially if any girl was brave enough to have a 'bunk-up' to hang over the wall directing proceedings! Of course the fight could always be continued on the way home and usually was, as there were many of us from the Bryant Road/Pytchley Road area at the school.

The discipline was very different then. On one occasion all the girls in our class were kept back in the playground after P.E. because someone had not pulled the chain in the girls' toilets. Our teacher at that time said if no-one owned up we would all get the ruler across the backs of our legs – and we did!

On Empire Day, towards the end of May, we all wore red, white and blue ribbons and assembled in the hall to sing 'Land of Hope and Glory', 'Rule Britannia' etc. and, of course, 'God Save the King'.

Our last year at Hawthorn Road was not spent in the school itself but, because of overcrowding, we were housed in St. Edward's Church Hall in The Grove – two classes, divided by a green curtain. The hall was dark, draughty and icy cold in winter. As there was no playground break time was spent in the old cattle market, where we played in the cattle pens, sometimes amongst the dead chickens, except on a Friday which was market day.

Despite all the privations we had to contend with we both have very happy memories of the time we spent at Hawthorn Road. One thing we would both be interested to know is whether the upstairs classroom with the big range and the tiered floor is still in use.

-- oOo --

From MRS. WARNES (1944-1950)

Mrs. Warnes was interviewed by Charlene Pell and revealed that she started school at 4½ years and found the set up quite frightening. She certainly didn't like the toilets as they were outside at the far end of the playgrounds. She remembers two Headmasters, Mr. Hudson and Mr. Bird.

She also remembers that school finished at 4.00 p.m. unlike today!

-- oOo --

From F.E. EVERETT (1946-1976) INFANT TEACHER, ST. PETERS AVENUE, KETTERING

I was very pleased to receive all the information about Hawthorn Road School Centenary. It is always Hawthorn Road School to me although I know that the 'Road' has been dropped from the name.

I was teaching in the Infants Department from 1946 until 1976 and I thought you might be interested to learn what is was like in 1946.

My class of 58 reception children was in the big middle room, it was billed to take a maximum of 80 children but fortunately it never did. The partition between my room and the next was opened every day for some joint efforts and was a real finger trapper and we were all very thankful when Mr. Woods had plasterboards put on both sides so it could not move any more.

The equipment in my room consisted only of a lovely big rocking horse, a large wooden engine on noisy iron wheels and a lot of natural coloured wooden bricks. There were also a number of broken bits of blackboard and when I asked the headmaster if we could have some whole ones, he collected the pieces up, got the top junior boys to work with the guillotines and I got them back straight edged but very small. If one wanted painting paper one had to apply to the headmaster who doled out the exact number of sheets that there were children.

Stretcher beds were used for half an hour every afternoon and were a perfect nuisance to put out and stack up again.

One great advantage of those days was the lovely big fire that was burning in the fireplace in winter months, and Mr. Laundon, the Caretaker, used to make it up every so often.

As you know the toilets were outside but there were terrible little basins in the lobbies. These had only cold water and that came from a <u>huge</u> tank in each tank room.

Incidentally, that is probably where the missing log books are, in the tank room. Everything for which there was no room always ended up in the tank room. As this water was unfit to drink, there was one grotty little drinking fountain in the playground.

There was a brick wall blocking off the infants passage from the headmasters stairs and the boys lobby and an iron fence which separated the infants playground from the girls playground.

Of course there was no canteen, lunch was served in the hall, and with tables to put up and take down, that was a nightmare!

I am thankful to say that after Mr. Woods came there was a vast improvement in just about everything.

I forgot to mention that neither teachers nor children were ever allowed to walk across the hall, in case the polish was spoiled. We all had to walk round the edge. Those were the days!

-- oOo --

From D.O. WOODS – TEACHER (1953-1973)

Many years ago the school toilet block was across the playground. The school had many, many pupils then and you can imagine the horror during a hard winter when everything was frozen.

Mr. Woods the Headmaster at the time, tried repeatedly to persuade the powers that be, to build new toilets within the school. All in vain however – there was never enough money. (I wonder how many times we have heard that?) and it wasn't a priority.

In those days, some thirty years ago, it was the custom to have Speech Days, when prizes were presented to pupils who had made the most effort, as well as to the high fliers.

113

Many eminent visitors came to do the honours. I remember a former Bishop of Peterborough and delightful Lady Hesketh, and many others.

During World War II Mr. Woods had served in the Middle East. He was working in the Education Corps, based mainly in Damascus and he had to explain the Beverage Plan to the troops. He worked with his friend Michael Stewart who became Labour M.P. for Fulham in Harold Wilson's Government. Eventually Michael Stewart M.P. became Baron Stewart of Fulham, but before he went to the House of Lords, he was appointed Minister of Education and eventually Foreign Secretary. What could be more appropriate than to invite an old friend, the Minister of Education to present school prizes? He stayed with us in Paradise Avenue. Can you imagine how those in authority reacted when they learned that the Minister of Education was actually coming to Hawthorn School and would be shown THE OUTSIDE TOILETS! Every obstacle to inside toilets being built, disappeared like magic. Never were plans drawn, approved and executed at such lightening speed!

Kettering Evening Telegraph

Helen Dickerson receives her Prefect prize during July 1958 from Michael Stewart, MP., Minister for Education in Harold Wilson's Labour Government

It is true that it isn't <u>WHAT</u> you know, but <u>WHO</u> you know that matters in this life – or am I being cynical?

-- oOo --

From JANET BANKS (nee PEASGOOD) BARNACK, STAMFORD (1955-1958)

I attended Hawthorn Road for just three years until 1958 when I left, aged 11 years. I do however have very happy memories of those years and few of those memories are of lessons! They are mostly of school outings: to the Royal Tournament in London (did the whole school really travel to St. Pancras on the train and then on to the Tournament by tube?); to Liverpool, taking a ferry across the Mersey! Also of the high jump practices in the playground prior to the town sports; counting and bagging up dinner money in small paper bags, before going to the bank (was there no school secretary?) The smell of boiled milk even today reminds me of the caretakers cellar – I'm not sure why, possibly though I was there washing up staff coffee cups!

There were Country Dancing Festivals, School Drama Competitions, Bird and Tree Competitions and more ...... but we must have done some work as I passed the 11 Plus. On the day we were told this good news we were each loaned 4 old pence to phone our parents from the Hawthorn Road phone box in order to tell them. I am not sure if those who failed had the same privilege though.

The Headmaster at that time was Mr. Woods. His wife also taught in the juniors, together with Miss Grudgings, Mr. Baxter, Mr. Scotney and one other male teacher.

-- oOo --

From MRS MARY ASHBY (nee MITCHELL) – TEACHER (1962-1987)

As Miss Mitchell I first joined Hawthorn School in January 1962 having worked for the previous two years at Northampton. My class was the first room in the infant corridor, a large room but containing more than forty of the youngest children. Each term some of the children were moved up to the next class and a new group of children started. There were no pre-school visits then and often the first morning was the child's introduction to school. The majority of the children stayed for school dinners from day one and this often caused problems and tears. However most children soon settled into the school routine.

I became Mrs. Ashby on my marriage in August 1962 and left Hawthorn School shortly before the birth of my daughter in July 1963. My son was born in 1966 and when he was two years old I was asked to take a junior class at the school for two weeks. This two weeks stretched into several months as the teacher I was replacing had severe back problems. Teachers were in short supply in those days, and for a number of years after that I did supply teaching at various schools in Kettering.

In September 1972 I rejoined Hawthorn as a full-time member of staff. By then the school was beginning to bulge at the seams and my first class was in what is now the remedial room (a rather large cupboard). There were twenty four, seven year old children crammed into it. The blackboard was fixed on the wall and I had to stand on a chair to reach the top of it. In January 1973 I became a reception class teacher again and my classroom this time was the canteen. About thirty children started school at 9 o'clock en masse, and at 11.30 a.m. we became refugees having to vacate the canteen so that it could be prepared for dinner. We either joined another class for singing or went into the hall. After dinner when the bell went at 1.30 p.m. we went into a shed known as the craft room, where the TV was situated and sat in our coats to see "Watch with Mother". If we were lucky we were reinstated in the canteen by 2 o'clock but the crashing and banging of washing up continued. Looking back I am often amazed that no one disappeared home when they went into the playground to go to the toilets in the main building.

In September 1973 I moved into what is now the kitchen/activity room and had a class of thirty reception age children there. It was small but bliss after the canteen. In the fullness of time I returned to my first classroom in the corridor, one of my favourite rooms. Over the years since I have taught in many of the classrooms in the main building.

As time went by, children and parents were invited into the school for pre-school visits and story times, this helped make starting school a less traumatic experience. Classrooms began to be updated and carpeted areas on

116

the floor were luxury, as prior to that we had to unroll bits of carpet at story time. As class sizes got smaller we were able to rearrange the tables to make a more friendly and sociable environment.

Over the last thirty years the world has altered a lot and the children of today have to be far more adaptable as they will probably have several changes of career in a lifetime. Computers in school were once quite a frightening prospect, but now they are just another helpful tool.

During my time at Hawthorn I have worked with three Headmasters: Mr. Woods, Mr. Findlay and Mr. Hall and many different members of staff. I have enjoyed my years at the school and have many happy memories of the children and my colleagues. I also remember with sadness the sudden death of Eileen Gerard an excellent teacher who had a wonderful fund of songs and poems, she had a fine turn of phrase and could always make you feel better.

I still enjoy working with young children as they are so enthusiastic and energetic, looking forward to the future. My own two children attended Hawthorn and have many happy memories but that's another story.

-- oOo --

From JACQUELINE SMART, WATTON AT STONE, HERTS (1963-1969)

Whilst rummaging through a box of souvenirs I discovered that I could remember quite a lot about my time at Hawthorn.

Each week "merits" were given out to the children who had done well. These were signed by the Headmaster, Mr. Woods, or at least bore his signature stamped in purple, as his own writing was very shaky. There was also a "demerit" system. I don't think that I collected any of these, as perhaps, my mother didn't keep them!

During the school year, there were various events: the Autumn fair, Christmas plays, school outings, prize giving, sports day etc. The sports facilities at the school were rather limited. We had a climbing frame and a scramble

117

net in the Broadway playground and a swimming pool near the canteen. To get to the Highfield Road sports field involved a long crocodile of green blazers with each child carrying a slipper bag. I remember clearly the egg and spoon, three legged, wheelbarrow, sack and obstacle races. Whatsoever the event the 1st, 2nd and 3rd were awarded ribbons, which could be worn for the rest of the week and these may be seen in some of the class photos.

On Monday mornings someone usually brought flowers for the nature table, or perhaps catkins, bluebells or a bird's nest and in the autumn we used to collect rosehips for Delrosa Rose Hip syrup. I think we were paid one shilling (five pence) for one pound of rosehips. The shop on the Argyle Street, Hawthorn Road corner was Taylors, who did a good trade in sweets at 3.30 p.m. each school day. We were happy to hand over 1 penny for four fruit salads or black jacks or 2 pence for a milky way.

There were 45 pupils in my class. I remember the homework in the top two years of the juniors – we were set IQ tests as practice for the 11 plus.

When I was in Mr. Scotney's class (4th year juniors) we started a weather station and my job was to measure the temperature of the swimming pool. All went very well until about two days before the end of the school year when disaster struck. I dropped the thermometer on a metal manhole cover and watched in dismay as the mercury ran away. This is my only bad memory of six years at Hawthorn – I hope the kids there now will be able to look back with as many happy memories as I can!!

-- oOo --

From PAUL AUCOTT- TEACHER (1970 – 1996)
To work in one building for over twenty years seems, on thinking about it, to be very dull and staid; yet it has seemed such a short time. I have very vivid memories of parts of that time and some of the people and personalities along the way and yet some is completely lost. The overriding feeling however is one of belonging and overall

contentment and that must be a good thing after a twenty year investment in ones work.

The morning I started at Hawthorn was very stressful. I had come from an open plan middle school, in a London overspill area, where everything had to be bargained for, repeated three times and co-operation between staff and pupils was nil. I was so glad to be in familiar surroundings in my home town and in a building similar to the one I had been educated in, which felt like a school. The bell was rung at 8.55 and then a teacher appeared and blew a whistle. The entire playground <u>instantly</u> stood still and silent – I couldn't believe my eyes. Class by class were called into the building and total silence remained all the way to the classroom.

The children walked in single file outside my classroom (the one next to the library) and I was pleased that there were only 36 not 38 as I had expected. We went in together, I to my desk at the front of the room and they to their rows of desks with hard wooden seats attached.

Thirty six children – nine in each house for stars or demerits. In those days we had four houses Buccleuch, Montague, Dalkeith and Gloucester which competed for stars. Nine stars meant a merit which was taken home with great pride. Three black stars meant a demerit and a telling off in assembly, also parents might be summoned to meet the headmaster! A demerit was the end of the world. (I know of somebody who remembers nothing about the year spent in my class except that he got a demerit, and he is 28 now!)

We took the register and I filled in the penny scheme book (where children brought a penny a week each for the purchase of class library books). Monitors were appointed for milk and tuck shop duties, also as I recall for clean-hand duty at dinner time and giving out and collecting books, cleaning the sink etc., so nearly everybody had a special job.

The timetable was devised by the headmaster and mornings would contain maths and English work. Maths was from a very complicated set of books called Alpha and

119

Beta for more or less able children. English was from Hayn Richards or English Progress Papers and silent/group readings were highly valued but not recorded in record books. Handwriting was also a very highly prized skill with much attention paid to it. Children virtually all wrote in pencil with only a few "good" 4th years using dip pens in inkwells on their desks.

All staff were expected to do a dinner duty in the canteen for which you received a free lunch. These were cooked on the premises by a rather formidable lady cook and three assistants who had been there since the place was built and who you kept on the right side of if you wanted a decent meal! The noise was tremendous in the concrete and asbestos building and it was never a great pleasure to eat lunch. The lunch hour was from 12-1.25 p.m. and school finished at 4.00 or 5.00 if you were a "bus child" and caught a special school bus to take children up onto the Hall Lane/West Furlong estates.

The afternoons would contain history/geography, band (Mrs. Watson's orchestra was renowned, having violins / drums / flutes / recorders / bass / violas and she would rewrite and orchestrate popular chart music or show music for the group and would plan regularly for fetes and festivals in the area), art / painting / sewing and games. Mr. Scotney was in charge of all sports and he seemed during the summer months to be constantly testing children for some athletic event or other and a vast array of silver ware seemed to adorn our school shelf for swimming and town sports and all other (now frowned upon) competitive events.

Of course the summers seemed longer and the weather warmer as it always does in hindsight. When I look back at those twenty years and see children of the children I first taught coming to the school I am proud to have been part of their lives and they of mine. We are above all a happy "family" school; where, despite minor arguments and upsets we all get along very well. As a staff we have still the ability to laugh at ourselves and as teachers, see that we only play a small part in the education of our pupils and that it is as a union with parents, society and each other on the staff, that we achieve what we have

120

always tried to achieve, happy confident, self motivated children!

People often harp back to a supposed "golden age" when standards were apparently higher and the children of Britain were "better educated". Of course it was different twenty years ago but taken overall I cannot say it was better. I have been fortunate for twenty years to be surrounded by sane and balanced colleagues and happy, confident and well motivated children. That wasn't just luck, it involved twenty years hard work, and I wouldn't have missed a moment of it.

During the next twenty years that I have left before retirement, I haven't a clue how things will develop in education or society. No doubt the changes will be as momentous as they have been in the past twenty years; but I am quietly confident that Hawthorn will be able to face the challenges with confidence, determination and humour and who knows, may be I shall still be here teaching the grandchildren of my first class – and they will not know their tables and get into a state over the complexities of long multiplication and they will still be making me laugh and cry and keeping me young at heart – I hope so!

-- o0o --

From PETER FINDLAY – HEADTEACHER (1974-1984)
Momentarily I felt it was very unfair! Here was I, sitting at the base of the letter 'T' green baize table being interviewed for the prestigious post of Headteacher at Hawthorn Road School at the old Divisional Education Office at 10 Headlands.

Managers, as they were then, lined both sides and the 'top table' comprised Inspectors, representatives from Northampton, the Divisional Education Officer and the Chairman of the Education Committee. A member from the top table leaned forward and asked, "Mr. Findlay, what do you consider to be the most important thing in a primary school?" "Thing" mark you! What was I to answer? All eyes were riveted on me as they had been during a long, and for me, exhausting interview. My mind raced through

121

the subjects. I paused for a very long time before I made my decision. "Happiness", I said. Consternation!! Then slowly, smiles and nods from practically everyone round the table. Happy smiling faces at the breakfast table show an eagerness to find out what the teachers have organized for today. I still believe that.

At the beginning of January 1974 we had 495 children on roll and, I think, 18 staff overall. There were two big mobile classrooms outside the girl's entrance and two classes being taught in the canteen, with a dividing screen. These classes had to move into the hall at 11.30 a.m. for reading groups or other activities whilst "the big lads" from 4th year set out tables and chairs on white painted marks on the canteen floor. Those dinners cooked on the premises were delicious, but when the price went up, it became containers brought to school about 10.45 a.m. Incidentally, 4th girls used to assist the infants, cutting up their meat etc.

The staff were superb and worked as a team. I felt it was my job to use their strengths, so apart from the school being academically very well thought of, we also became highly acclaimed in music, with splendid school concerts and wonderful contributions to the School's Music Festival and also annual drama productions. I know, parents, they were the hardest seats in Kettering! We also became Northamptonshire Primary Chess Champions two years running and kept a high profile in netball, soccer and field and track events at the Town Sports. It would be unfair to mention members of staff involved because everyone, yes everyone, buckled to and helped in so many ways. Just to say that in my 10½ years at Hawthorn I received from all of them the utmost support and encouragement for which I was, and am, most grateful.

Many of you will remember that St. Mary's CE Primary, where I was previously Headteacher, developed serious cracks in the Autumn Term of 1973. It was eventually demolished of course. When I had been at Hawthorn for about a fortnight in January 1974, I had an urgent message from Mrs. Tidball's classroom beyond the swimming pool. I rushed round. "Mr. Findlay, we can see the bushes and the fence through the classroom wall!"

They could too, through two big cracks! When I rang the Department in Northampton, a man said "1974 re-organisation Mr. Findlay, we're just moving from the old Guildhall Road HQ to our new beautiful offices. Don't come anywhere near us will you?" A lovely sense of humour.

Sometimes Northampton forgot to tell headteachers what they planned for their school. We had a lovely tree near the canteen and one lunch time I drove my car carefully from the Broadway gate, through the children to my parking place. The tree had gone! Sawn off, six inches from the ground. There, standing by the stump was dear Miss Everett, with a face like thunder. She was always kind and courteous. That day, before striding away, chin high in the air, she looked me straight in the eye and uttered one word, "VANDAL". (It seemed later that there was a condemned tree at another school!!)

One cannot put ten years or so of fun, or indeed tragedy, which we encountered together in one article, it would need a book. But I would thankfully put into one word my time with children, staff and parents. Happiness!

-- oOo --

From CAROLE GOODLEY – HAWTHORN ROAD VISITOR (C.1990)
On arrival – just before nine o'clock – I reported to Mr. Hall's office, where he told me what to expect of a usual Wednesday assembly.

I was given a seat around the edge of the hall with the staff who accepted my presence as a usual occurrence; it was the children who eyed me with suspicion and who, when Mr. Hall enlightened them, promptly lost interest. Lines of children filed into the hall to the calming influence of some classical music, small at the front, older ones at the back. Mr. Coleman began, then handed over to Mr. Hall who, between hymns, managed to capture the attention of the hoard long enough to impart some words of wisdom about parent's fear of allowing their children to go out on their own for the first time. This was followed by the handing out of swimming certificates and other awards to the applause of their class mates. Assembly concluded with some more music selected by Mr. Coleman for it's calming quality but turned out to be Whitney Houston at full blast – it nearly had me up on my feet and dancing, never mind the rest of the school! A somewhat bemused (or was it confused) Mr. Hall managed to restore order and return everyone to their classes.

Miss Wingrave gave me a warm welcome and introduced me to the children. After a few minutes the attention of the class returned to their cross seed experiments, which they were far more interested in. Afterwards the children re-grouped into three tables of about eight; I joined the group that was doing writing practice and drawing. Again they were not disturbed by my presence and carried on with their work. The more outgoing ones spoke to me and I spoke to the quieter ones. As usual, the girls did their work without too much chattering whilst the boys seemed to have more to show off about. I told them if they really wanted to impress me they should finish their work before the girls. This was obviously good ploy – within minutes they were finished".

At break time I was invited for coffee in the staff room. The fifteen minutes flew by hardly giving anyone time to take a breath before returning to class. I explained to Miss Wingrave a little about the greeting card business and how I usually spent my day – it seemed like a life of leisure by comparison.

Mr. Hall found me again and this time escorted me to Mrs. Dix's class, which consisted of a mixture of year two and three. The room was a bit like an upstairs broom cupboard and I only just managed to fit in. I had to admire the use of space; there were children up a ladder in one corner, a few in a quieter room next door and the others filling the more usual places around tables. This class was working on various projects concerned with living things, and was happy to explain what they were doing. The boys knowledge of sharks and dolphins was quite daunting – I could hardly keep up the conversation! Finally I had a chance to speak to, a much in demand Mrs. Dix, and congratulate her on her handling of such a lively group. Then it was time for lunch – phew!

As Mr. Hall had said before my visit, and which I can now happily confirm, this school is a very open, happy and visitor friendly environment with lots of visual stimulation and both children and staff who are highly motivated. The morning passed very quickly leaving my head reeling with all that I had seen. I realised, more than ever, what a wonderful job was being done.

PS. Thank you for having me.

-- oOo --   -- oOo --   -- oOo –

Chapter Eight

Some Hawthorn Headline Makers

Chris Bambridge (centre – referee) with Gordon McQueen (right) and Ian Bowyer prior to the Manchester United –v- Notts Forest game at the MCG Melbourne on 3 June 1984. A game which Manchester United won 1-0

I have traced a number of former pupils whose details I include within this Chapter. Unfortunately no females will be found here. I tried to flush out a number of contacts but without success.

There are obviously many female ex scholars who would fit into this Chapter very well and I only hope that they surface before the next book is produced about Hawthorn, so that then they may be included!!

-- oOo --

Featured in this Chapter:-

Chris Bambridge	1954 – 1959
Matthew Bell	1982 – 1989
Bill Bellamy	1932 – 1933
Peter Hudson	1928 – 1935
Brian Reynolds	1937 – 1943
John Ritchie	1946 – 1953
Robert Ritchie	1956 – 1963
John Robinson	1935 – 1939
Terry Sumpter	1937 – 1943
Sonnie Torlot	1941 – 1948
Terry Wright	1936 - 1938

-- oOo --

Chris **BAMBRIDGE** (1954-1959), Liz **BUTLIN** (1953-1959)
Both Chris and his wife Liz attended Hawthorn and I include
details, with grateful thanks that I received (by email) from them,
of their schooldays.

Subject: Goodday from downunder

Carl

My sincere apologies for not responding sooner
Hope it's not too late
We have searched through bags of photos and albums in
the hope of finding any school photos without success but
will keep looking.
Have tried to open the old brain cells to see what we can
recall of Hawthorn Road School

- *Liz (maiden name Butlin) went from 1953 to 1959*
- *Left St. Gabriels in 1964, went to London for 12*
  months then returned to Kettering (and me).
- *Chris started 1954 to 1959*
- *Then onto Stamford Road Boys School*
- *School had 4 "Houses" Buccleuch (Green); Gloucester*
  (blue); Montague (Red), Dalkeith (Yellow). Both Liz
  and I were in Buccleuch.
- *School colours were green and yellow (close to*
  Australia's) and I recall a bottle green blazer and cap
  with yellow piping.
- *School sports were held on Highfield Road playing*
  fields, where Liz always excelled, and I used to
  regularly win the "Egg and Spoon Race"
- *Some teachers we recall were **Miss Grudgings**, **Mr.***
  Bob Scotney** (also played rugby for the town), **Miss
  ***Everett, Mr. Burkhill**,. We believe the Headmaster*
  *was **Mr. Woods** and that his wife taught at the*
  school too.
- *Pupils I recall are **Nicky Burden** (his Dad was the*
  *town librarian), **Alan Lomath/Edwin Kendrick***
  (both lived off London Road on the right hand side
  *down in the hollow, Springfield Road?), **Robert Ellis***
  *(brainiest kid at the school) **Richard Arden/Philip***
  ***Jones** who all lived Headlands end of Broadway,*
  ***Ian Parsons** who married an Aussie and emigrated*

to Sydney in 1971/2 and I met up with him in the mid-70's but have lost contact (his Dad was the Bursar at Kettering Grammar School when it was in Bowling Green Road), **Jean Larcombe** *(had an older sister named Ponty?)* **Isobel Caswell, Roger Abraham** *(who lived in Argyle Street and was later team manager of Revellers, the Sunday League team I played for),* **Alan Thompson** *(1 Garfield Street).*

- *Liz recalls a girl who was at the Home and a couple of years older,* **Edith Woodruffe***, now Skillman who lives in Barton Seagrave.*
- *If we think of anything or anyone else we will be in touch.*
- *Sending football CV separately*

-- oOo --

Whilst not exactly setting the soccer world alight with his Sunday performances with the Revellers, Chris had started along what turned out to be a most successful path towards becoming a world class soccer referee. It all began with tuition and discussion at the home of Ray Toseland who was then the Coaching Officer of the Kettering and District Referees Association and at that time was a Football League linesman. Chris' course was over eight weeks and then he passed an oral examination to be let loose in the Youth League for a game or two, in order to put theory into practice, under the interested gaze of Bill Draper, a local "referee watcher".

Prior to 1974 when Chris and Liz emigrated to Australia, in addition to Youth League games, Chris had also officiated in both the Kettering Amateur League and the Kettering Sunday League. From this point Chris had kindly sent me a summary of his progress in Australia.

Chris Bambridge – Summary CV

Current: Football Federation of Victoria Referee Development Manger *(since 2001)*

Achievements:
- *Active referee from 1971-1991.*

129

- *1977-1991 Referee in various forms of Australian National Soccer League (incl. 3 Grand Finals) Retired after 1991 Grand Final.*
- *1981-1991 Referee on FIFA referee's list (see below).*
- *1997-2001 President Soccer Referees Victoria (formerly ASRF Vic)*
- *2000 inducted into Soccer Australia "Hall of Fame".*
- *Since 2001 as full-time Referee Development Manager FFV and FFV State Referee Coach, referee numbers have grown from 301 to 1007.*
- *Accredited Level 1 and National League Inspector*
- *Accredited Level 2 Referee Coach.*
- *Member of National Referee Coaching Panel.*

FIFA Achievements:

1981   FIFA U23 World Youth Championships (Australia) – Assistant Referee Panel

1983   FIFA U23 (Mexico) – Referee Panel

1984   Olympic Games ASIA final Qualifying Tournament (Singapore) – Referee Panel

1985   FIFA U17 World Cup Finals (China) – Referee Panel (and referee of the Cup Final)

1986   FIFA World Cup Finals (Mexico) – Referee Panel

1988   Olympic Games South Korea – Referee Panel

In addition, refereed 40 other "A" International matches with Australia and Oceana, including World Cup and Olympic Qualifiers.

To close Chris's story on a humorous note, David Thorpe writing in the Evening Telegraph of 21 February 1986, when Chris had been appointed by FIFA to officiate in Mexico during the World Cup Finals, mentioned Joan (Chris's mother) who was then and definitely remains, a fervent Poppies supporter, "well known" (he wrote) "for her vocal treatment of opposition goalkeepers". When reading this Ray Toseland commented:

David Thorpe has got that wrong, Joan is well known for giving me (as a referee) the verbals, from behind the Rockingham Road end goal at Kettering – and I only helped train her son!

130

There's gratitude for you!"

-- oOo --

Matthew **BELL** (1982-1989)

I heard about Matthew and his hammer throwing exploits in a very round about manner, almost third hand as it were. I did however eventually track him down and he kindly supplied me with the following summary of his athletics career so far (which is quite impressive I must admit), together with his aspirations for the future.

I started Hammer throwing in 1990 being coached by Gordon Binley, who was the National Under 20's coach for the event and luckily he was based at Corby Athletic Club where I competed for 13 years, before leaving to go to my current club of Birchfield Harriers.

My main achievements to date are as follows:

I competed in the English Schools Championships in 1992, 1993, 1994, 1995, 1996 and 1997 gaining four medals in total, (two bronze, one silver and one gold).

I was the British champion at the under 17, the under 20 and under 23 levels.

I was also in the Great Britain Team for the under 20's and the under 23's competing in over 20 international matches within Europe.

I am the most successful Hammer Thrower in the history of Northamptonshire, holding county records at under 17, under 20 and at senior age group levels.

I am currently the County and Midland champion and am also ranked 6th in the UK overall and hope to be the UK champion within the next few years.

My main aims for the future are to compete in the 2010 Commonwealth Games in Delhi and then hopefully to compete in the 2012 Olympics in London and other major championships.

So, let us all look out for Matthew in the future and hope to see him enjoy success in the 2012 London Olympic Games and bring home a gold medal for England, for Northamptonshire and indeed for Kettering Hawthorn Community Primary School.

-- oOo --

Bill **BELLAMY** (1932-1933)
Bill first came to Hawthorn during 1932 when he was eight years of age. He admits to having little recollection of school work but certainly remembers the Sports Day when he came fourth in the potato race and second in the relay (blue ribbon!). He also writes of enjoying rounders and country dancing with partner Hilda Knight.

He remembers a kindly Miss Cawston, whom he likens to Joyce Grenfell (I can certainly recall resemblance in size and shape – C.H.) and he also remembers Peter Hudson, a boy he much admired, who lived in a large house close to Wicksteed Park. Bill had a special friend at school named Ruth who sat at the next desk. He still retains a severe conscience about this young lady as the pair marked each others test paper in class. His was 100% correct, as was Ruths. Bill, however, altered one of her answers to make it wrong! He cannot remember her speaking to him again!

Miss Jarvis was his class teacher and she had even taught his Aunt Edna, before him.

Bill and his friends had bicycles and he used to ride home to Roundhill Road to his Aunties for lunch each day. He also spent quite some time on his cycling expeditions farther afield with one very good friend Michael Swain.

Bill went from Hawthorn direct to Blackfriars School, Laxton during September 1933. He joined the Royal Armoured Corps at the end of 1941 and was commissioned out of Sandhurst early in 1943, joining the 8th Kings Royal Irish Hussars in North Africa, as a regular officer. Through contracting dysentery, coupled with recurrent jaundice Bill was discharged from the Army in 1955 with the rank of Captain.

He had married Ann Burbury in 1950 and they had five children. He served throughout the northwest Europe campaign in 7th Armoured Division (the Desert Rats), landing in Normandy on D Day plus three and entering Berlin as a member of the initial occupying force during July 1945. He fought the campaign as Troop Leader in Cromwell tanks and was awarded the Military Cross in Holland in November 1944. He then served for three years on the staff of an Armoured Brigade, returning to the UK to become Adjutant, firstly of his own regiment and then through health reasons, Adjutant of the Northamptonshire Yeomanry. During his wartime service he maintained a diary which he turned into a book in 1945. This was published in 2005 as "Troop Leader". He is currently working on a second book describing life in Kettering during the 1920's and 1930's.

Bill Bellamy receives his Military Cross from Field Marshall The Viscount Montgomery of Alamein during November 1944

Bill Bellamy Collection

He joined Phipps and Son Ltd. in Northampton in 1955, becoming Group Managing Director during 1959. He followed this by becoming Group Managing Director in a joint company with W.W. Chamberlain & Co. Ltd. Retiring in 1983, he became Chairman of Mayday, a local charity. He worked with the Northampton Museum authorities to create a Northamptonshire Yeomanry room within the Abington Museum. He is currently involved with a number of other charitable pursuits, including the Cynthia Spencer Hospice. Bill's wife sadly passed away in 2001, but he does enjoy the company of his five children and seventeen grandchildren!

Bill does add, most coincidentally, that during his Army career he came across Peter Hudson, who was at that time serving with First Battalion of the Rifle Brigade in Germany, but he had no idea that he was the very same Peter Hudson whom he had known at Hawthorn Road School many years previously!

-- oOo --

Peter **HUDSON** (1928-1935)
Peter was the son of Captain William Hudson, the Headmaster of Hawthorn during the 1930's and 1940's. During his years at the school, Peter lived at the family home of Lea Hurst, Pytchley Road, Kettering. He was later educated at Wellingborough School from 1936 until July 1942. He was very active in school life becoming a Prefect in 1941; 2nd XI cricket 1940; 1st XI cricket 1941; Vice-Captain 1942. He played for the Colts soccer team 1937/1938; 1st XI 1941. Rugger 1st XV 1942. He became Hon. Secretary of Garne's House 1939-1942. School athletics team 1941. Drum Major in the band 1941 and Sergeant Shooting VIII 1941.

Wellingborough School Collection

Peter Hudson front row, second left, Wellingborough School Colts Soccer XI. 1937-1938

During late 1944, after completing his degree in maths at Jesus College Cambridge, he was commissioned into his fathers regiment, the Rifle Brigade. During 1955 he was in action in Kenya against the Mau Mau terrorists and later saw further action against the Chinese backed guerillas in the Malayan emergency. Following his success in these campaigns he was then appointed as Brigade Major to Bernard Fergusson who had served with the

134

Special Forces. He was Military Assistant to Quarter Master General, Sir Charles Richardson, at the War Office between 1963 and 1966. These appointments gained him valuable experience and provided the 3rd Royal Green Jackets with a top-class Commanding Officer, previous to his taking command, during 1968 of 39 Brigade in Northern Ireland prior to the civil rights movement erupting into serious violence. By this time he was a Freeman of the City of London.

After attending Imperial Defence College, he was promoted Major-General and became G.O.C. Eastern District. In 1975 he moved to Oslo as Chief of Staff of the Allied Forces in Northern Europe. On promotion to Lieutenant-General he was appointed Deputy Colonel-in-Charge United Kingdom Land Forces (1977-1980) and in 1978 became Inspector General of the Territorial Army.

Upon retirement in 1980 he remained involved with the T.A. as Chairman of the Council of T.A. and D.R.A. and later as President of the Reserve Forces Association. His other posts included Secretary-General of the Order of St. John (1981-1989), member of the BBC Advisory Council (1981-1985), Lieutenant of the Tower of London and Deputy Lieutenant of Berkshire.

The Hawthorn Road School old boy retired from the Army as Lt.-General Sir Peter Hudson, gaining an MBE 1965; CBE 1970; KCB 1977.

Sir Peter died in Reading, Berkshire on 8 August 2000, just a few days short of his 77th birthday.
(With many thanks to the Independent Newspaper – August 2000)
-- oOo --

Brian L. **REYNOLDS** (1937-1943)
Born 10 June 1932 in The Oval, Kettering

Brian played first class cricket for Northamptonshire for twenty years in well over 400 matches. He totalled almost 19,000 runs and was considered at his peak, one of the top opening batsmen in England. He topped 1,500 runs in five consecutive summers during the early 1960's, and was seen as a truly dedicated professional. Following his first class playing career, he spent thirteen seasons as Chief Coach in charge of Northamptonshire 2nd XI and a further eleven years as Cricket Development Officer. Looking at this record it is perhaps not too surprising that John

Arlott wrote of Brian, *"In his own mind he is not only a cricketer, he is a Northamptonshire cricketer."*

Brian is still a regular visitor to the Wantage Road ground in the Summer, with his charming wife Angela, except of course when they are on one of their cruising holidays, which they love so much.

As an allround sportsman Brian also played soccer for Kettering Town F.C. and Peterborough Utd. He later qualified as a referee.

B. REYNOLDS
Northamptonshire

John Watson Collection

Kettering Evening Telegraph
John Ritchie

-- oOo --

John **RITCHIE** (1946-1953)

To quote Ian Addis (Licensed Crank, E.T. 24th March 2007) who was a contemporary of John Ritchie, *"I can recall nothing of his footballing exploits as a schoolboy or youth"*. It therefore appears that John was a comparative late comer to competitive soccer, as he learned his football in the Kettering Amateur League. The late Albert Smith, well known and well loved amongst the elder generation of Kettering sportsmen, is recorded as supporting and advising John along his road to success. Big John was first signed by Kettering Amateurs after he was seen playing football in Wicksteed Park, but being employed by Munn and Feltons in Wood Street, he was persuaded during 1958 to join the works team Emmaneff . During 1960 Jack Froggatt realised his potential and

136

signed John for Kettering Town. He made his Southern League debut on 12 December of that year when he netted his first goal for the Poppies, against Merthyr Tydfil. He went on to score 40 goals in 76 appearances for Kettering Town which of course attracted the Football League scouts to the Rockingham Road ground.

He moved on to Stoke City for a fee of £2,500 during 1962. Emmaneff receiving a donation of £10 from Kettering Town Football Club in recognition of the sale!

In his debut game against Bolton Wanderers he scored twice to establish himself in the Stoke City first team, alongside a true legend, Sir Stanley Matthews. When Sheffield Wednesday, during November 1966, came in with a bid of £80,000 for John, Stoke City could not afford to turn them down. So John spent three years at Hillsborough, netting 35 goals in 89 games for Wednesday. Tony Waddington, the Stoke City Manager, realising that he had made a mistake in selling John, bought him back in 1969 for £27,500 to play in the same team as a second soccer legend, the great Gordon Banks, who was the then goalkeeper at the Victoria Ground.

Glory, in the shape of the League Cup came John's way in 1972, when Stoke City beat Chelsea 2-1 at Wembley. On the downside that year however, John was sent off a mere 29 seconds after coming on as a substitute against Kaiserlautern of Germany in a UEFA cup tie.

Tragically a double fracture of his leg, suffered against Ipswich Town during September 1974 eventually forced his retirement from the professional game at 33 years of age. He did play a few games, however later for Stafford Rangers during 1976, a non-league club for whom younger brother Bob played with some distinction for some time.

Following football, John ran a pottery business near Stoke for some years until 2003 when he was forced to retire due to ill health.

Sadly he passed away at the end of February 2007, aged 65, leaving his wife Shirley, two sons, a daughter and several grandchildren.

137

Robert **RITCHIE** (1956-1963)
Although not making quite the impact on the English soccer scene, as his older brother John, Bob Ritchie was more than a useful performer on the non-league scene during the late 1970's, as Kettering Town found during 1979.

Nick Andic Collection

Robert Ritchie, front row second left with teacher Bob Scotney and The Hawthorn Soccer Team of 1961

The Stafford Express and Star Newspaper

Robert Ritchie back row extreme left, Captain of Stafford Rangers Football Club. F.A. Trophy Winners 1978-79

Obviously well nurtured in the Hawthorn Road County Primary 'A' XI during both the 1961-1962 and 1962-1963 seasons by Sports Master Bob Scotney, Bob Ritchie, in 1979 was the proud skipper of Stafford Rangers F.C., (following spells at both Arsenal and Stoke City), when they beat Kettering Town 2-0, at Wembley in the final of the F.A. Trophy. I remember the occasion only too well as I was there amongst a crowd of 32,000 with my ten year old son Mark, supporting Kettering Town. Little did I know then that the Stafford Rangers skipper had followed me, albeit some 14 or 15 years later, through the classrooms and playgrounds of my old school! So possibly the result was not as bad as I first thought, for there was a compensating factor!! A lad from Kettering, an old boy of Hawthorn Road School had lifted the trophy from soccer legend Billy Wright at Wembley Stadium on Saturday afternoon 19 May 1979!!

-- oOo --

The following excerpts taken from the eulogy of John Marshman **ROBINSON** (1935-1939) were found on the web-site of the English Chess Federation and they were written by David Ingyon, John's next of kin and cousin.

John was born on 31 July 1931 at Kettering and was the only son of Clare and Frederick Robinson of 47 Hawthorn Road, Kettering.

He was accepted for a place at Kettering Grammar School at the age of eight years and having been endowed with the brains in the family John made steady progress gaining a school certificate in eight subjects followed by a higher certificate in pure and applied mathematics, physics and chemistry, being then awarded a place at Birmingham University. His extra–mural activities involved the debating society, fell walking, public reading, photography and chess. He was certainly academically orientated rather than sport. From a young age he was taken regularly to the Lake District by his parents where they all enjoyed the magnificent scenery and walking, giving him the foundation to trek through the Austrian and Continental mountains, subsequently spending time in the high peaks of Nepal. On the 26th February 1995 he added the ascent of Mount Kenya (over 16,000 feet), reaching Point Lenana, to his achievements.

Having been directly involved in the County of Northamptonshire he was then invited to become an umpire on the national chess circuit. Having demonstrated his abilities and fairness he was eventually assisting in the organisation of international chess championships and was appointed to the prestigious official position as an international chess arbiter and called upon to oversee matches and tournaments in such places as Hastings, The Isle of Man, Moscow, Armenia, Istanbul etc.

John became an important part of the British Chess Team and was congress secretary for some years. His work on the laws of the game in the mid 90's has left its mark – being incorporated in the laws in present day use. Rewards came in the form of the prestigious Boxall Salver for his work with the British Championship Team and the President's Award for Services to Chess. For many years John gave his time and enthusiasm in order to teach youngsters how to play and enjoy the game at Rushton Primary School where, I'm told his presence and humour will be sadly missed. As, indeed, it will be, in the local community where he became Church Warden of St Peters Stanion, during 1994 taking an active interest in projects and works concerning the repair, restoration and renewal to the fabric of this fine building of Christian worship, I'm told he also made very good currant cakes!! Other activities in which he took an active part included swimming, bridge clubs, musical evenings, photography and inter – village quiz team competitions.

Although feeling poorly and somewhat incapacitated with what he though was a slight stroke he persevered and tied up all the immediate existing matters in the chess world that he was dealing with before submitting himself to be taken by his church friend Ken Gibbard to Kettering General Hospital. An extensive analysis of his condition revealed that in fact he had tumours of the brain which proved to be advanced and untreatable.

Doctor Perera and staff played a very important part in making sure, through their efforts, that John's last days were as comfortable and pain free as possible.

*His friend David Welch, Manger of Congress Chess &
Chief Arbiter from Liverpool, states on the English Chess
Federation website:-*

*"I have never met a person so genuine and dedicated as
John Robinson, it has been a privilege to know him"*

-- oOo --

Terry **SUMPTER** (1937-1943)
Terry's memories of his early school days are quite clouded, but
after leaving Hawthorn, he went first of all to the Parish Church
School and then on to the Central School. His working life began
as a chemist at Cransley Furnaces and later at Stewart and Lloyds
at Corby. He was called up into the Grenadier Guards and from
there to the Parachute Regiment.

His Police career began in 1955 with Northamptonshire and
covered eleven years service at Kettering, Wellingborough and
Corby, including a 6 month detachment to Birmingham with the
Regional Crime Squad.

He then applied successfully to Leeds City Police for a transfer as
Sergeant and worked with them until March 1974, when the Force
was merged with others to become known as the West Yorkshire
Metropolitan Police Force until March 1986. It was then re-styled
West Yorkshire Police Force and Terry, then a Superintendent,
stayed on until retirement during December 1992.

He had spent 37 years devoted service to the community during
his Police service, as his commendation well noted!

-- oOo --

Sonnie **TORLOT** (1941-1948)
Sonnie and I were at Hawthorn during the same period. We started
school on the same day and in fact spent quite a time within the
same class, throughout our school life. I remember him as rather a
quiet lad, who when we were in Mr. Payne's class, in our final year
(the upstairs classroom), he sat in the row next to the window and
spent a great deal of time looking out, much to teacher Alan
Payne's chagrin.

141

He moved on to senior school and then took up brick laying and house building. Over his life he has built many houses and was one of those people who tended to rather irritate me, as he could turn his hand to anything. Whether it was plumbing, electrics, plastering, car repairing, reading music, the lot! He did have problems keeping his lawn cut however!

Sonnie and his sax

He became infatuated with the saxophone from the age of sixteen, from one Saturday evening spent at the Drill Hall, Wellingborough, listening to the then local top band of the day, Vic Riches and his Orchestra. He began to take lessons and just after being called up for National Service within the RAF, he set up his first band, "The Jets", playing rock and roll. He also played the saxophone in an RAF military band.

Following National Service, he continued playing and setting up various bands, and when one had run its course, he would start up another, still playing his rock and roll favourites. During 1983 he joined "Lost Weekend" and played with them for twelve years, the longest period that he had ever been involved with one band.

However prior to this, the highlight of his musical career came when he was playing with "Coast to Coast" and decided to feature a song called "Do the Hucklebuck". The song was duly recorded and the record rose to number four in the top twenty best selling singles during 1981. (Barry Manilow was number five) and stayed in the top twenty for nineteen weeks! Sonnie was presented with a gold record by his record company Polydor, for selling half a million copies worldwide. Indeed total sales were only 150,000 short of one million, it really was a great hit! "Coast to Coast" toured Europe, including Germany, Denmark, Norway and Ireland, being greeted by large crowds and rapturous applause. The downturn however was whilst playing in Belfast, on May 5th 1981, the stage was stormed and taken over by a number of voluble supporters of Bobby Sands, the IRA hunger striker, who that night in the Maze Prison had passed away on the 66th day of his hunger strike. They were seeking publicity for the IRA cause and Sonnie remembers that the situation on the stage became quite scary. Needless to say the band flew home shortly afterwards.

Whilst the record was at number four, there were various T.V. appearances, and I remember Sonnie and the band playing their song on the Little and Large show, which then enjoyed a peak weekly Saturday evening T.V. slot. At that time Sonnie and I had by pure chance purchased houses opposite to each other in Cedar Way, Wellingborough and I was quite disappointed that I didn't spot any "groupies" outside his house, as I had offered to help him with any such surplus!

"Coast to Coast" produced a follow-up record, "Jump the Broomstick" which Brenda Lee had sung some years previously. Sadly this number only reached 27 in the hit parade, so the fame started to dwindle somewhat.

"Coast to Coast" split up sometime afterwards and Sonnie has not had a regular band for several years, preferring to help out old friends and fill-in, as required. He is so well known in the music business that he is always playing somewhere. For example during May 2007 he "guested" for the "Question Marks" at a most successful week in Skegness, but for sometime now (June 2007) he has carefully been setting up and rehearsing a brand new 10 piece Boogie Woogie Swing Band which includes a 6 piece brass section and a piano, playing late 1940's swing music. So look out world, we could have a big hit on its way once again from a Hawthorn Road old boy!!

-- oOo --

Terry **WRIGHT** (1936-1938)
Terry became a Kettering Borough Councillor in the days prior to local councillors drawing an attendance allowance – when candidates stood for the pleasure of serving their community

without the benefit of financial reward! He initially represented the Labour Party within Pipers Hill Ward during 1966, then with ward boundary changes served the electorate of St. Marys Ward until 1979, when following a further boundary change he lost his seat after 13 years of Council service.

He does say that he and his Council colleagues throughout his public service were annoyed by the continual erosion of Local Authority power due to Government interference so in that sense he was not too disappointed at losing his seat.

He particularly enjoyed his twelve month term, 1977-1978, whilst representing Kettering as Mayor. During this time Terry and his wife Molly as Mayoress, attended over 400 events. He met many townsfolk and discovered that there were over 120 organisations within the Kettering boundary, some of which he had no previous knowledge, but they nevertheless all went about their chosen works in a quietly efficient way!

Terry opened the Edgar Newman Chapel within the local crematorium grounds during 1977 and was pleased to open the rebuilt St. Marys School in Fuller Street during November 1977 also. He officiated at the Newborough Centre during the same year when it first became operational, with a mere handful of working shops. The Centre however, did enjoy a second, possibly more official opening the following year, by the then Mayor Councillor Cecil Brown.

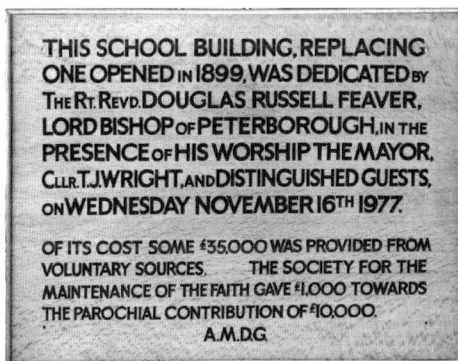

THIS SCHOOL BUILDING, REPLACING ONE OPENED IN 1899, WAS DEDICATED BY THE RT. REVD. DOUGLAS RUSSELL FEAVER, LORD BISHOP OF PETERBOROUGH, IN THE PRESENCE OF HIS WORSHIP THE MAYOR, CLLR. T.J. WRIGHT, AND DISTINGUISHED GUESTS, ON WEDNESDAY NOVEMBER 16TH 1977.

OF ITS COST SOME £35,000 WAS PROVIDED FROM VOLUNTARY SOURCES. THE SOCIETY FOR THE MAINTENANCE OF THE FAITH GAVE £1,000 TOWARDS THE PAROCHIAL CONTRIBUTION OF £10,000.
A.M.D.G

D.L. Photography

The major highlight of the civic service of Councillor Terry Wright was surely in being invited along with Molly to the Buckingham Palace Garden Party during the Queen's Silver Jubilee Year, where they met the Queen Mother. "*A Super Lady*" he remembers!

144

Should the reader ever find themselves in the company of ex-Kettering Town Councillor T. Wright, may I suggest that one subject to keep clear of might be "the destruction of more old buildings within the Kettering boundary".

Terry expresses very strong feelings against those who have destroyed part of Kettering's heritage and who appear hell bent in pursuing a policy of destruction, in the name of progress, in the future.

Terry was a useful soccer player at Hawthorn and later played Town League cricket for many years, both with Kettering British Legion C.C. and with the Glebe C.C.

-- oOo --   -- oOo --   -- oOo --

Chapter Nine

The Out of School Club and Playschool

The Hawthorn out of School Club consists of the

Breakfast Club

After School Club

and the
Holiday Playscheme

The Playschemes run with at least two members of staff at any one time, each with suitable experience for the post.

The Playschemes are registered with Ofsted and adhere to set policies.

If you are interested in any of the above please contact **Kim Cullington on 0781 347 8205** or collect an application form from the School Office or download from the School Web Site WWW.HAWTHORNCOMPRIM.IK.ORG

Hawthorn Out of School Club

General Information

D.L. Photography

HAWTHORN Out of School Club commenced activity in the year 2000. Initially it comprised two parts, the After School Club and the Holiday Play Scheme.

The After School Club which caters solely for Hawthorn pupils, each school day from 3.15 p.m. until 5.30p.m. now offers toys, puzzles, craft activities, outdoor play including soccer, badminton and tennis in a happy environment. The children cannot go hungry either, as drinks and sweets or savoury snacks are made available within the modest charge.

The Holiday Play Scheme operates, as we may possibly guess, during school holidays, normally between 8.30a.m and 5.30p.m. (Monday-Friday). Should children need to be dropped off earlier (from 7.45a.m.) breakfast may be arranged if necessary.

Children are expected to bring along a packed lunch but will in addition be offered a drink, together with a snack, both mid-morning and mid-afternoon.

A variety of activities are on offer, both indoor and outdoor, from toys and puzzles to playstation, dance mat, craft activities and computer. Whilst outdoors, badminton, tennis, basketball and soccer may be enjoyed.

During September 2006, following the success of the first two schemes, the school saw fit to launch a Breakfast Club. It was decided to open up on school days for pupils from 7.45a.m. All attendees had to be pupils of Hawthorn and would be handed over to the school at 9.00a.m. each day, having been offered options of cereal, yoghurt, eggs, fruit, bagel, croissants or milk shake for breakfast, with which to start their day.

The Breakfast Club children would be looked after within the Community Room, where all the usual activities would be available.

During 2003, Kim Cullington who started working with children over twelve years ago (1995), as a Learning Support Assistant and is now a Higher Level Teaching Assistant, became the Manager of the whole "Out of School" operation. She has a core of seven permanent qualified staff and may call upon a number of suitable students when the pressure and numbers build. For example during the 2006 summer holidays, more than 100 pupils (not all Hawthorn) took advantage of the excellent facilities of the Holiday Play Scheme to enjoy themselves within the confines of the school.

The three schemes are of course registered with Ofsted and enjoyed a most favourable last report from the Inspector, as they naturally adhere quite strictly to the national policies that apply to such arrangements. For example, at least two members of staff, each with suitable experience, are required to supervise the children at any one time.

All three schemes are accountable via Kim Cullington to Head Teacher Richard Hall and the School Governing Body and as a consequence are required to be totally self-funding.

The charges (from April 2007) for the three schemes are as follows:

Breakfast Club	-	£4 per pupil per session
After School Club	-	£6.30 per session
Holiday Play Scheme	-	There are seven variations on available sessions and prices vary from a Full Day Session beginning at 7.45a.m. (which includes a full breakfast) until 5.30p.m. at £20.00, to a morning or Afternoon Session (from 9.00a.m. and 1.00p.m. respectively) for £8.50. The school office of course holds all the details for interested parents.

-- oOo --

Jacc Batch

Playschool children 1997 with teachers Faith Walker (left) and Sue Brown

148

The Playschool

The Playschool is run totally separately from the Hawthorn Out of School Club and has now been operating for some 15-16 years, growing from two sessions per week to a maximum capacity of ten per week.

At the moment Carine Fritz supervises the Playschool which enjoys the benefits of national funding for five staff, the odd casual worker and general expenses.

Twenty four children can be accommodated during morning sessions and a similar number in the afternoon, within the Playschool's own mobile premises.

The financial arrangement is that currently the parents foot the bill up to the childs third birthday, whilst after that time the parents are usually in receipt of nursery funding.

There is certainly no copper bottomed guarantee, but playschool children are usually offered a place in the Hawthorn Infants School when the time comes.

There is a certain financial benefit to the main school, as the Playschool currently provides around £8,000 net profit per annum which is directed to the coffers of Hawthorn Community Primary School.

-- oOo --   -- oOo --   -- oOo --

Chapter Ten

The Headteacher Writes

By

Richard Hall, B.A., Dip.Ed

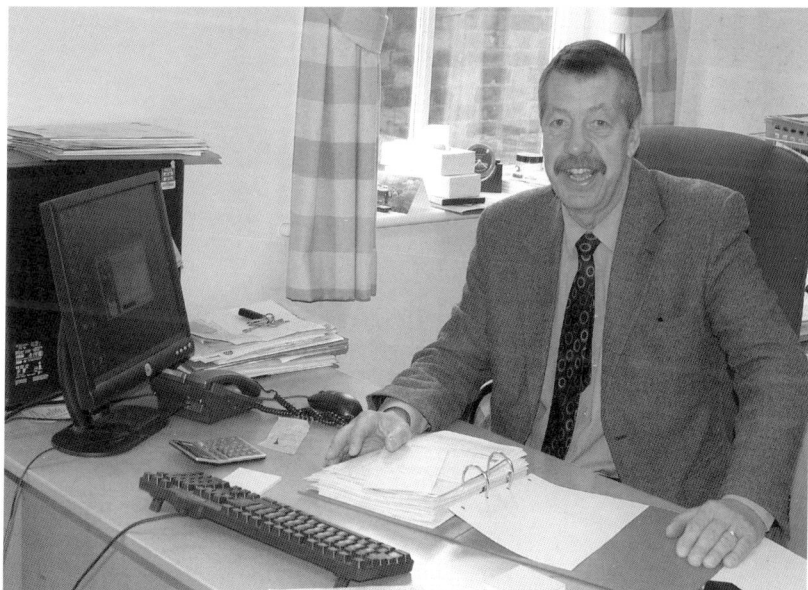

D.L. Photography

ON April 5th 1984 I attended an interview for the post of Headteacher at Hawthorn School. According to my predecessor (Mr Peter Findlay) the interview panel was, as stated in Peter's entry in the school log book, the highest powered ever assembled for a school other than for a secondary school. That so many worthy people should have gathered together, considered all applicants and then offered the post to me fills me with amazement!

That they did of course gave me my first and only experience of Headship, for here I remain until I choose to retire. Those of us old enough to remember will know that the world of 1984 <u>was</u> different. The school building I walked into in 1984 was dark, dingy and 'tired', the building I now walk out of, whilst being structurally very similar, is bright, warm and welcoming. This transformation, if that is the correct word for a twenty four year odyssey, is due to many things not least luck, hard work, opportunism, Parental Support and (not least) Local Management of Schools.

Back in 1984 there were 242 children on roll in 9 classes. There were nine teaching staff in addition to the Headteacher.

Within weeks I became aware that the school had no money to spend so whatever ambition I had (and I had lots!) to improve the learning environment was likely to be thwarted. Within months the National Union of Teachers, in support of an ongoing pay claim, imposed restrictions upon what teachers should do. These restrictions included not attending staff meetings. This, somewhat bizarrely, was the trigger for what became (and remains) my commitment towards improving the environment in which children are to be educated.

With no staff meetings and no curriculum initiatives to worry about, the hammer and the saw became the pre-eminent tools of my trade. Assisted by the then school caretaker, we set about ripping down pin boarding which served only to make the building dark, removing cupboards and the stage from the school hall and many other practical improvements to the building. The problem of having no money to spend was eased when I discovered 'HT orders' which allowed the Headteacher to authorise minor repairs and maintenance works costing less than £50.00. Amazingly, thereafter, there were so many broken windows and damaged toilets to be repaired that a closer scrutiny of the goings on might have aroused suspicion!

Toward the end of the 1980's we encountered both Local Management and the introduction of the National Curriculum. It is my opinion that Local Management (LMS) is the very best that ever happened to schools. Suddenly, there was presented to us, funding which properly reflected the number of pupils in our school as against a system which was externally driven and not always fairly so. In the early years of LMS we were disadvantaged because the transition from existing (historical) funding of schools to LMS operated against those schools with increasing pupil rolls (and in 1991 this school was accommodating 283 pupils). Notwithstanding that problem, LMS afforded us the opportunity of determining our own staffing structure and targeting ongoing improvements to the building. In 1984 the then school secretary and the one school ancillary (so called) shared 40 hours. Today we have 50 dedicated hours within the school office and employ 20 support staff who work in excess of 300 hours per week within the classroom environment.

The immediate advantages of the National Curriculum are much more difficult to recollect! The merits or otherwise of the National Curriculum in its first draft were most notable for the vast, and I do mean vast, volumes of paperwork for each curriculum area. During those days both the rainforests and the poor teachers were razed to the ground, one in the demand for paper and the other by government expectation!

We humans do have the capacity to adapt to our environment however and slowly, slowly, sense was made of successive revisions of the National Curriculum and now, it should be said, the framework does afford shape and direction to what is taught in schools.

Yet more was to follow of course, if schools were to have a National Curriculum the Government required some mechanism for judging how effective it was and so OfSTED was born. OfSTED...... the Office for Standard in Education was given teeth and (seemingly) a succession of Chief Inspectors who liked to bite. Such startlingly bad newspaper headlines as *'70% of Headteachers are inadequate'* or *'1 in 4 schools failing'* bombarded the psyche of the general public. It must be assumed that by both popular opinion and pupil

152

numbers Hawthorn School is not thought to be failing but my own credibility remains in doubt perhaps!!!

As a school we have tried not to be too driven by a results agenda, believing as we do, that children deserve a rich and stimulating curriculum. This view may, of course, not be in tune with the criteria by which OfSTED measure schools. Increasingly a school inspection relies upon a data analysis of progress in English and Mathematics which can "persuade" schools to devote increased resources to those limited areas of the curriculum at the expense of others. Because we have not been "persuaded", the pupils of Hawthorn School have benefited from a lovely and lively curriculum. Of course children do need to read, write and numerate and the many successful young adults who were once in attendance at this school are evidence that the basics of education are equally properly addressed.

Over the years I have had the good fortune to work with many committed and capable members of staff; many, many enthusiastic and talented children; made contact with scores of very supportive parents and worked in tandem with interested and interesting governors. All of these groups and many individuals have helped to shape the ethos which now so defines our school.

In other chapters of this book mention is made of the evolution of the Hawthorn Playschool and of the 'Out of School' Club. These aspects are now part of the school, not by chance or circumstance, but because the seeds of such provision were created and then developed into a practical reality. And, it might be added, these extra facilities to our school were effected well before the government began to promote the vision of 'extended schools!' Part of the government's agenda for extended schools is to provide *out of school care,* to enable more parents to go to work. Our vision was born of a different virtue, that schools are and therefore should be at the very heart of the community.

The word 'community' is central to our philosophy. Our school is both a community and within a community and as such all of us have some responsibility for the effective partnerships which must exist if the school is to be successful.

Others have a right to judge our effectiveness but we do strive to develop within our pupils a sense of moral responsibility, tolerance, respect for self and others and compassion. I am of the belief that the vast majority of children who attend this school are happy and well looked after and take with them, when they leave, good memories of a lovely school.

The school building has continued to improve. The addition of the Early Years Area, an area often greeted with admiration or envy by visitors, ensures that our youngest pupils are so well catered for. The Community Room hosts the Breakfast Club, After School Club and the Holiday Play scheme and serves many other useful purposes. In 1984 the Headteacher's office was upstairs and next to it was a small cupboard which the school secretary occupied. The re-modelling of the school ensured that the 'existing' Reception Area was adjacent to the main door rather than up a flight of stairs above the boys toilet.

The Cabin was erected and this oak framed wooden building replaced the old play barn which had operated as the Swimming Pool changing room for so many years. In their enthusiasm to get changed for swimming the children perhaps never noticed how awful these changing rooms were! The cabin also serves as our ICT suite, the existence of which confirms our desire to keep up to date with the electronic age in which we live.

During the 1990's and to the present the school developed a wonderful (and I would boast-rarely paralleled) reputation for musical performance. The first such performance, Oliver, was staged at the McKinlay Theatre in 1991 and in the words of one parent at the time 'made an albatross of expectation around our necks'. If we might have been worried then, the track record of musical success in the intervening years has well and truly buried that bird! Subsequent blockbuster productions have included The Wizard of Oz (twice), Bugsy Malone, Oliver (again), Rats and most recently Joseph and his Amazing Technicolour Dreamcoat.

Harvest Festivals, Christmas Productions, School Fayres and much more characterise schools but such is their continuity at Hawthorn that they all fit like well worn slippers! Many charities have been supported and many, many thousands of pounds have been raised by the Parents' Association which is and has been invaluable for the purchase of additional resources.

In 1985 maybe the first ever school residential visit took place and since then, every year, the older children in school have had the opportunity to attend a residential experience. Since 2005 we have organised three such trips a year to cater for children aged 7 years and above.

Ian Jones drawing of Hawthorn Road School courtesy of Helen Jones

In the future former associates of Hawthorn School may read this extract and perhaps expect to read about particular members of staff. To list them all would be nigh on impossible and to list some risks the wrath of those who have been omitted! Here though I do wish to record my particular thanks to those current and former colleagues who, by virtue of their enthusiasm, commitment and vision, have made a difference to how things developed in this our Hawthorn School:

-- oOo --

My sincere thanks to Richard Hall for providing this Chapter
(C.H. November 2007)

-- oOo --   -- oOo --   -- oOo --

Chapter Eleven

The Governors with Martin Moloney

Could I become a Governor Guvnor?

WHAT does a School Governor do? How does one become a Governor? Who can stand for election as a Governor?

It is probably fair to say that most parents are not too concerned about the Governors of their children's school. In fact, they probably don't even know their names. Yet, it has to be in the parents (and the childrens) own interest to know who the Governors are and what they stand for, as according to their deeds, these Governors can have a great influence on the children in our schools.

Below we see details of becoming a Governor and what is expected from a Governor at this time (July 2007).
(With thanks to Northamptonshire County Council and their website
for the information)

-- oOo --

D.L. Photography

The Ian Blackwell drawing of Hawthorn School

What does a Governor do?

Governors are responsible for working with the head teacher to think strategically about how to raise standards of achievement for

157

all pupils at the school, for setting the budget and for overseeing the curriculum.

Governors will:
- promote high standards of educational attainment;
- set targets for pupil achievement;
- take general responsibility for the conduct of the school;
- manage the school's budget, including deciding how many staff will work there and their pay;
- make sure that the curriculum is balanced and broadly based, in particular that the National Curriculum and religious education are taught, and report on pupils' achievement in National Curriculum assessments and examination results;
- participate in the appointment of senior staff (including appointing the head teacher) and regulate staff conduct and discipline.

Why do schools need governors?
Every school has a Governing Body to represent the public in the running of schools. School governors bring perspectives from ordinary life and work with the staff and the Local Authority to help secure the best possible education for the children in the school. They have important responsibilities such as managing the school budget, overseeing the curriculum and appointing staff.

Are there rules for running a governing body?
There are no terms of reference or regulations that a governing body has to adhere to. The governing body determines its own terms of reference. There are Terms of Reference Regulations which clarify the prospective roles of both the head teacher and governing body.

Governing bodies must act as a corporate body. They must also act with integrity, objectivity and honesty and in the best interests of the school. They must be open about, and prepared to explain, their decisions and actions.

The governing body should carry out their functions with the aim of taking a largely strategic role in the running of the school. This includes setting up a strategic framework for the school, setting its aims and objectives, setting policies and targets for achieving the objectives, reviewing progress and reviewing the strategic framework in the light of progress. The governing body should act as a "critical friend" to the head teacher by providing advice and support.

The head teacher is responsible for the internal organisation, management and control of the school; and for advising on and implementing the governing body's strategic framework. In particular, head teachers need to formulate aims and objectives, policies and targets for the governing body to consider adopting; and to report to the governing body on progress at least once every school year.

-- oOo --

Selection criteria for becoming a Governor

I declare that I am aged 18 or over and the following statements are true:
1. I do not already hold a governorship at the same school;
2. I am not liable to be detained under the Mental Health Act 1983;
3. I am not a member of the governing body of more than two schools (excluding ex-officio governors, temporary governors, or additional governors at schools causing concern);
4. I am not an ex-officio governor specified in the instrument of government of more than two schools;
5. I am not a bankrupt or subject to a disqualification order under the Company Directors Disqualification Act 1986 or to an order made under section 429(2)(b) of the Insolvency Act 1986;
6. I have not been removed from the office of a charity trustee or trustee for a charity by an order made by the Charity Commissioners or the High Court on the grounds of any misconduct or mismanagement or, under Section 7 of the Law Reform (Miscellaneous Provisions) (Scotland) Act 1990, from being concerned in the management or control of any body;
7. I am not included in the list (List 99) of teachers and workers with children or young persons whose employment is prohibited or restricted;
8. I am not disqualified from being the proprietor of any independent school or for being a teacher or other employee in any school;

9.   I have not, in the five years prior to becoming a governor, received a sentence of imprisonment, suspended or otherwise, for a period of not less than three months without the option of a fine;

10. I have not, in the twenty years prior to becoming a governor, been convicted as aforesaid of any offence and has had passed on me a sentence of imprisonment for a period of not less than two and a half years;

11. I have not, at any time, had passed on me a sentence of imprisonment for a period of not less than five years;

12. I have not been fined, in the five years prior to becoming a governor, for causing a nuisance or disturbance on education premises;

13. I am not subject to a disqualification order under the Criminal Justice and Court Services Act 2000.

In making decisions on the appointment of LA Governors the following criteria needs to be met:

•   Has a commitment to, and an interest in, education;
•   Has a desire to support the school concerned;
•   Has a willingness to serve the local community;
•   Has skills and experience which will support the work of the school;
•   Has the ability to work as a member of a team;
•   Is able to arrange their commitments to fit in with membership of a governing body;
•   Will respect the Council's views on education matters at governing body meetings.

-- oOo --

Governing body profile

The composition of governing bodies varies between school categories. Between March 2003 and 31 August 2006 all school governing bodies had to choose and adopt a new constitutional model.

In this new framework the size of the governing body can range from a minimum of 9 to a maximum of 20 (this can vary for voluntary aided schools). Within this range each governing body can adopt the model of their choice, provided it complies with the guiding principles for their category of school.

These principles prescribe which categories of governor must be represented on the governing body and what the level of representation is for each category.

Categories of Governors

- Parent governors - parents, including carers, of registered pupils at the school are eligible to stand for election for parent governorship at the school. Parent governors are elected by other parents at the school. If a parent works at the school for more than 500 hours in a school year, they are not eligible to be parent governors. If insufficient parents offer themselves to fill the number of parent governor vacancies, the governing body may appoint any parent of a child under compulsory school leaving age;
- Staff governors - teaching and support staff paid to work at the school are eligible for staff governorship;
- LA governors - appointed by the LA (Local Authority);
- Community governors - appointed by the governing body to represent community interests;
- Sponsor governors - appointed by the governing body;
- Associate members - appointed by the governing body.

-- oOo --

Having read through the theory of Governorship I felt that I should compare it with the "real" or "practical" side of the position. I arranged a chat with Kate Webb the current Chair of Hawthorn Governors, but as she had been in the post merely a matter of weeks, she felt that possibly she wasn't the proper person to deal with my research. She very kindly pointed me towards Martin Moloney who had served a total of twelve years as a Governor of Hawthorn School which included eight as Chairman. Interestingly his time had covered the School Centenary period, so I felt that a chat with Martin could prove to be doubly useful!

The initial approach proved most successful and Martin most kindly produced his thoughts in writing, entitled "The Governors Perspective", which I am delighted to produce here in full, with my most grateful thanks for his efforts.

-- oOo --

161

The Governors Perspective

The governor is the school's "critical friend".

This is the maxim taught in governor training and promoted by the more recent writing on school governing. It is the guide that I certainly have used throughout my twelve years as a governor of Hawthorn School.

Like many school governors, I was initially attracted to governing as a way of becoming more involved in the school attended by my own children; and as a member of the Labour Party, I was given the opportunity of being nominated as their sponsored governor at the school.

One of the first things I found out was that the position of governor gives you, if anything, less influence over the treatment of your own children as the ethos of governing is that the position is not to be used for personal purposes but is a service to the school and the Local Education Authority (LEA).

With the help of a training programme provided by the Local Education Authority, I quickly learned that governors are there to support the school staff, to help develop longer term strategies for the school and to keep a watchful eye, ensuring honesty, legality and probity.

I first joined the Governing Body in 1992, when Monica Eastwood was Chair. It was a strange and confusing experience getting to grips with not only how the school worked – curriculum, finance, discipline, personnel etc. – but also how the governors fitted into all of this. It soon became clear that the governors had a sort of parallel system of committees to oversee all the different aspects of school life and that governors would then be in the position to ask the necessary questions to ensure that policy was being followed and standards were being met.

It soon occurred to me that we, the governors, were actually the bosses of the school, in part responsible for proper function and answerable to the LEA and ultimately to the National Government. That put things in perspective.

162

However, for all the apparent power and responsibility we held, it was clear that executive power was firmly with the head teacher who ran the school like the captain of the ship. That was another perspective – the Admiralty in London may be in charge of the navy but the captain definitely runs his own ship.

But responsibility aside, my memories of those early years are dominated by getting to know the school better by joining in activities, sitting in lessons, and generally being around the school absorbing whatever was going on.

As I gained confidence, I joined some of the active committees that made up a lot of the governors work. This included the Finance Committee – Chaired ably and knowledgably by Clive Standen, though however many times I attended the meetings I have never really got to fully understand those balance sheets!

One of the main drives in those first couple of years was the impending Centenary of the school. After much discussion involving governors, staff and the parents and friends of the School, it was decided that we should aim for something practical and lasting as a symbol of a hundred years of providing education for the local community. We therefore settled upon building an "annexe" hall to the school which would enhance the functioning of the school while also acting as a resource for local community groups.

Although this was finally budgeted at just over a hundred thousand pounds, we learned that we could access substantial grants from Local Government and other sources – provided we could demonstrate our own commitment by raising a significant proportion of the cost ourselves. Thus the fund-raising committee was set up – consisting of staff, governors and those veteran fund-raisers, the Parents and Friends of Hawthorn School.

Through a myriad of schemes and projects, and not a little begging from local and national charitable schemes we raised a five figure sum (the exact figure eludes my recall), and over the following months, the community annexe

163

arose and was finally formally opened by Phil Sawford,
Kettering's Member of Parliament.

By this time, I was the new Chair of Governors – Monica
Eastwood having retired after six years as Chair. My
relationship with school became much closer as I tried to
have a good overview of the workings of the school and
properly discharge my duties as Chair of Governors.

Over the nineties, the role of governor evolved quite
considerably. When I first joined the Board in 1992, the
governors seemed to have little direct involvement in the
day-to-day life of the school; but new legislation gave new
responsibilities to governors – particularly around ensuring
standards and goals were met and in taking a more direct
role in the strategic development of the school and its
relationship with the local community.

Richard Hall, the head teacher, and I met frequently and
regularly and, I believe worked very well together to steer
the school through the development projects from the
bricks and mortar of the place to curriculum developments.
As I pointed out above, there was no doubt who ran the
school, but the collaboration, co-operation and support of
the governors ensured that the goals and the process were
in line with National Government and LEA requirements
and that all decisions and actions could be defended from
a legal and moral basis.

One of my own aims as Chair of Governors was to make
the working of the Board a bit more transparent; governors
are often seen as remote and insular by the parents. We
already had five governors elected from the
parents/guardians group, and particularly their regular
presence in the playground was immensely helpful.
However, parents would tend to approach usually when
there was something to complain about, which could
encourage a negative relationship between the parents
and the governors. To keep parents informed on a wider
basis, we initiated a regular newsletter – following the
main governors' meeting each term. In this I would
describe the outcome of each issue raised at the meeting
and its relevance. I don't know the relative proportion of
"read" to "binned" (and indeed to "found in a screwed up

164

mess at the bottom of the rucksack six months later") but I hope it gave at least some parents a greater insight into the running of the school – and indeed into the greater part they may play in it.

We also had occasional surveys regarding ideas for school improvements that parents and children might like to see and also the obligatory yearly parent's and governor's meeting. The latter was so poorly attended every year, whatever incentives were offered, that it was a blessed release when this was declared no longer mandatory by the Department of Education. However we liked to believe that the lack of interest was mainly because of a general satisfaction in the running of the school.

The governors' meetings were an essential part of the process of discussing and approving (or rejecting) new projects and ways of assimilating new initiatives from the Department for Education. In our Board, we aspired to a concensus approach to decision making whenever possible, and I do believe that in my whole time as Chair, we never had to actually vote on any issue – logical argument having swayed the group as a whole.

These meetings could be a bit tedious at times by the formal nature of the business, so every governor was encouraged to have their own area of responsibility – curriculum areas, health and safety, staff issues and so on – so that every member was involved in some way.

We also initiated a second termly meeting when very little business was discussed, but the time was devoted to learning about some aspect of school life – be it academic curriculum, the key stage system and marking, arts and sport in the school, or staff training. The underlying aim was that if we have a group of lay people making important decisions about the school then they should be as highly aware of the realities of school life as possible.

Although I had an excellent relationship with Richard Hall, the head teacher, and enormous respect for his running of the school, I believed that the important role of Chair of Governors should move through different hands to avoid stagnation and complacence. Consequently, after eight

165

years in the post, I decided it was right to move on and allow someone else to take up the baton. I believe that, during my tenure, the governors provided the balance (and ballast) to keep the ship of Hawthorn School steady and balanced as it sailed its course into the new century. I think of it as a job well done and much enjoyed.

Martin Moloney - October 2007

-- oOo --   -- oOo --   -- oOo --

Chapter Twelve

The Parents and Friends Association of Hawthorn School

By

Alison Bagley

During the 2002-2003 year the PFA provided refurbishments, renewals and fittings to the value of £6,000 for the benefit of the School and the pupils, from funds which it had raised.

HAWTHORN School Parents' and Friends' Association has been going for as long as anyone can remember. The reason why it was formed is no doubt the same reason we're still going today, fundraising and fun for the children by the parents.

Initially the Parent's Association the PA became the PTA to include Teachers. Due to it's popularity the PTA was expanded to cover 'friends' too. Even when their child has left the school ex-parents still come along to help at the events.

Although running in the days of Mr Findlay a 'new' PA was instigated by Head teacher, Richard Hall. He wanted parents to be more involved in raising funds for school. On the original committee Richard Busson was elected chairman alongside Pat Bickle, Jenny Wareham, Maureen Fuller, Judy Barney (in her pre-teacher days), Joan Busson, Liz Mortimer, Caroline Phillips, Sue Rodwell and Richard Hall.

In the early 1980's the PTA had the big fundraising fair in the autumn term. Crafts and games made by children and parents set out on market stall style tables. At Christmas the children came in fancy dress and had their Christmas party in the old school canteen at the back of the school. Another hugely popular and highly anticipated event was the end of term panto. In the days when there was a stage in the school hall the teachers would perform for the school such shows as The Snow Queen and Annie.

Some things haven't changed in over 25 years. Jumble sales, discos and providing the drinks at sports day are still things done to this day. Other aspects aren't all that different either. Richard Busson remembers the terrible time when all the takings from the Christmas Fair were stolen during the night. Burglars broke in through a skylight and jemmied the office locks. In 2006-7 something very similar happened to the 'cabin' where the 12 brand new lap tops paid for by the PTFA were stolen during the holidays. The next funding went to a security system to make sure it didn't happen again.

One of the tastier fundraisers was The Hawthorn School Recipe Book. Each family gave away their culinary secrets for inclusion in a book. This guide to domestic success is still used to this day by former committee member and classroom assistant Liz Mortimer.

Unfortunately, food of a different type ended up in court. Richard Busson remembers when the Hawthorn barbecue party to be held in the school playground caused objections from the neighbours. A licence application for the Entertainment Licence (for two barrels of real ale) meant a court hearing! It was touch and go whether the licence would be granted. Richard Busson had his morning in court and got the thumbs up.

As I write in at the start of the Autumn Term 2007 I can see from the Treasurer's report that in the last year we raised over £ 4,000. Say it quickly and you might not even notice the amount but to raise that sum we have an excellent team of dedicated volunteers willing to give their time, planning and running events.

Each term we try to run two main events one just for the children and a family friendly thing.

In winter we have our ever-popular Christmas Fair. Santa always makes a visit and makes his home in the library grotto. Snowball skittles, Splat the Pat, Sing-a-long-a-carol singing, mega tombola and anything with to do with chocolate.

The Summer Fair is a moveable feast. It gets called the May Fayre, the Spring Fair, the Midsummer Fair, the 'It's Not Fair Fayre' and takes on various guises to suit our chosen theme. This year was an old fashioned fun fair which included a coconut shy, fairground organ, stocks and home-made sweets.

In 2008 the fair will be on July 4th and will inevitably have an American theme.

In past years we've dressed up as Victorians and flowers, pirates and clowns and the children have come in fancy dress.

We've had an ice-skating rink, sleep-overs (for the kids), wine tasting (for the grown-ups), a conker championship, a race night, several fashion shows and many excellent barn dances.

Our jumble sales have quite a following. It's incredible just how much stuff everyone finds to stock two massive jumble sales a year. It's a tough job manning the bric-a-brac stall with a punter quibbling over 5p. In these days of ebay everyone is on the lookout for a bargain to sell on.

169

With cakes being sold at every possible occasion and whenever possible and the fantastic teddy tombola, a way of recycling those pesky soft toys when you donate three teddies and win five ("Oh that's nice darling." You say as you sneak them out of their bedrooms).

All these fantastic events are there for us as parents and friends to support the staff at Hawthorn School in their goal to educate, stimulate and empower our children. Politics aside, if we had as much money as we wanted we would still never have enough. It's a sad reality that we have to raise money for necessities. But we don't really have any choice. We also provide for some of the little extras.

When the Community Room was built the PTFA played their part in the funding of the project. Without the support of the parents this now integral part of the school would not exist. Everyone who hires the room for a party or comes to mums and tots is benefiting from the fundraising expertise.

So we'll carry on with the fundraising ideas for 2007-2008. Plant sales, tuck shop, second hand uniforms, fun mats, calendars, mobile phone recycling, tea towels and I'd really like to try that Hawthorn recipe book idea again.

My sincere thanks to Alison Bagley (Chairman of Hawthorn Parents' and Friends' Association) for providing this snapshot of the P.F.A. – CH November 2007)

-- oOo --

Subsequent to Alison producing the above, I learned from Jane Watson (School Secretary 1989-2005) that there has been a Parent-Teacher Association at Hawthorn since 1955. When it first started on the 30th March 1955 virtually every child at the school was represented at the meetings, as Mr. Woods, the Head Teacher at the time, expected a full house and nobody would have liked to have been seen to let him down.

The meetings arranged in the early days covered many topics, with speakers coming into the school to talk about their particular subject, sometimes to inform or educate the parents, other times to talk about their experiences or interests. Although some fund raising took place (a small subscription was asked to become a member) it was very much a liaison group, keeping parents and staff informed of the topical items of the day. With all members very keen to help the school, when money was required to enhance the facilities at the school there would be many volunteers with fund raising and also practical help with the task.

-- oOo --

It is evident that with the combined efforts since 1955 of parents, teachers and friends, the School has been greatly improved in many, many ways. The PFA has cause to be extremely proud of its continuing efforts to enhance School life, over the past 50 years and more.

-- oOo --   *-- oOo --*   *-- oOo --*

Chapter Thirteen

A Closing Miscellany : Action Photographs with news items from over the years

The All Action Maypole Dancers

SOME of this material has been found within school scrapbooks, some has been taken from various minutes of the Kettering Urban District Council Education Committee and sub-committees, whilst the remainder has been provided from a variety of other sources.

The coloured photographs were taken during September 2007 by D.L. Photography with very many thanks.

-- oOo --

Kettering School Board 4th Triennial Report 1899-1902 indicated that in singing, the children of Hawthorn Road School showed a great tendency to lower the pitch. Frequent scale practice might be helpful.

-- oOo --

The Kettering Education Committee in its report about Hawthorn 1902-1903 indicated "creditable progress is being made, but the organisation is defective. Classes should not be taken in the passage".

-- oOo --

Hawthorn Road School report minuted 27th January 1902 includes "discipline might be smarter"; "handwriting is crude in character"; "needlework is very good".

-- oOo --

<u>Estimated Expenditure on School Maintenance</u>
<u>30 September 1903-31 March 1904</u>

	£	
Salaries	150	
Bonus	10	
Materials	14	
Prizes	2	
Gas	1	
Firing	5	
Water	1	
Repairs	5	
Caretaker	13	
Rates	14	
Furniture	5	
TOTAL	220	For the half year period

K.U.D.C Education Committee Minutes 1904

-- oOo --

174

February 1904. Miss E.A. Clarke (Headmistress) was at the top of her salary scale at £130 p.a.

-- oOo --

Mary Ashby remembers Marjorie Wardle, who was a Hawthorn pupil during 1905, telling of classes of 80 children in the Infants School (*possibly two classes with the partition pulled back – C.H.*) and the teachers were assisted by the older children from the Junior School coming in to help teach the infants!

-- oOo --

School Management & General Purposes Sub-committee minutes of Monday 12th February 1906 reveal that Mr. Cartwright had received an application for admission to Hawthorn from a boy in the union workhouse. The application was granted but was not to be treated as a precedent.

-- oOo --

The Sub-committee unanimously approved a pay increase from £1 to £1.3.0d per week for Mrs. Z. Cooper the Caretaker, at their November 1906 meeting.

-- oOo --

The School Inspector's report to the S.M. & G.P. Sub-committee at the meeting on Monday 17th December 1906 indicated that it had been pointed out, more than once, to the Headmistress (Miss E.A. Clarke) that the timetable should be strictly observed, especially in the final closing of the registers and also in the punctual dismissal of the children. He regretted that he again had to call attention to the non-observance of these important regulations, which if again reported might endanger the grant.

Meeting of School Management & General Purposes Sub-Committee of Monday 14th January 1907 – A letter relative to H.M. Inspectors report, from Miss Clarke was read and referred to a special sub-committee.

Miss Clarke resigned from 31st May 1907

The meeting of 6th May 1907 was advised that 40 applications had been received for Miss Clarke's job. Miss Clapp of Birmingham was to be appointed Headmistress at £100 p.a. to commence 1st September 1907.

-- oOo --

The Committee unanimously agreed with a suggestion from Mr. Cartwright that the boys be allowed to wear a school cap for which the parents would be expected to pay: July 1907.

-- oOo --

The Committee approved the appointment on 13th January 1908 of Mr. C. Cooper as Caretaker in place of his mother Mrs. Z. Cooper. The wage was to be £1.4.0d per week.

-- oOo --

10th February 1908. Mr. Cartwright reported that Mr. A.R. Brake had presented the school with a stuffed woodpecker in a case. The best thanks of the Committee were therefore accorded to Mr. Brake.

-- oOo --

	31.3.1905	31.3.1906	31.3.1907	31.3.1908
Average school attendance	125	260	286	333
Teacher salaries P.A.	£323	£509	£811	£881

-- oOo --

22nd July 1908. The School Inspectors report indicated "The work done in this school is of good quality".

-- oOo --

7th July 1911. The Board of Education had agreed to the proposed amalgamation of the infants and mixed departments of Hawthorn to take place later in the year.

-- oOo --

6th November 1911. Mr. Cartwright, Headmaster, to be paid £5 for extraordinary services regarding the amalgamation of two departments at Hawthorn.

-- oOo --

22nd January 1917. Mr. J.G. Gidney the temporary Headmaster received £10 for extraordinary services since Mr. Cartwright resigned on 24 November 1916. Mr. Gidney himself left Hawthorn on 18 February 1917 to take up a position at Lowestoft.

-- oOo --

May 1917. Owing to the pressing needs of woollen comforts for the troops, the Clerk to the Education Committee had been instructed to write a letter to the schools asking them to arrange for the scholars to take "knitting" during the needlework class to enable the local War Workers Association to execute the requisitions from the War Office as speedily as possible.

-- oOo --

September 1917. The Clerk reported that the Secretary of the County Education Committee, at the request of H.M. Government, had arranged for the county schools to undertake the collection of blackberries for making into jam for H.M. Forces and the question of Kettering schools participating in the collection had been raised. The Sub-committee resolved unanimously to request the head teachers to organise the collections.

-- oOo --

October 1917. Mr. C. Cooper, the Hawthorn Road School Caretaker, was to receive five shillings per week from the date of his absence on military service.

One month later the Sub-committee reconsidered the above decision and revised the amount to four shillings per week.

-- oOo --

Owing to an outbreak of whooping cough the school closed from 11th March 1918 until Easter 1918.

-- oOo --

Hawthorn was to be allowed to rent a school garden in the allotment field off the Headlands from July 1918.

-- oOo --

Mr. C. Cooper, Caretaker now demobilised, will restart 16th November 1919. Wages would be 32/- per week plus 18/- per week war bonus.

-- oOo --

The Sub-committee minutes of December 1921 indicated that the Hawthorn drainage and defective w.c's had been inspected. Consequently the w.c.'s were to be replaced! (*This appears to be the start of a problem that lasted on and off for some 80 years! – C.H.*)

-- oOo --

The Clerk was to write to Head Teachers during April 1923 instructing them not to dismiss pupils from school when thunderstorms were about.

-- oOo --

During May 1923 a very satisfactory report on Hawthorn was received from H.M. Inspector.

-- oOo --

During June 1924 Mr. R.B. Wallis presented the school with one of his works, Castle-an-Dinas.

-- oOo --

Miss Cox retired December 1924, she may now draw her pension.

-- oOo --

Kettering Urban District Council Education Committee, School Management and General Purposes Sub-committee extend to George Harrison their sincere thanks for the gift of an oil painting presented to Hawthorn Road School, which was formally hung on 22nd April 1926 in the School Hall.

-- oOo --

Miss Huckbody resigned from April 1929 to work in a missionary school in India. Miss Butler was appointed to replace her.

-- oOo --

Mr. Markham (Headmaster) pronounced unfit to continue working. To be paid until 28th April 1931.

-- oOo --

A letter from the Head Teacher asking for the erection of a flag pole to display the Union flag presented to Hawthorn by the Tasmanian School was read at the Education Committee annual meeting of May 1937. The Secretary was instructed to suggest that the Committee felt it better to continue to display the flag inside the school.

-- oOo --

At the Education Committee meeting of September 1939 it was indicated that under the Government Evacuation Scheme, 80 girls from Bartrams Convent School (under the L.C.C.) were to be absorbed in Hawthorn Road Junior School.

-- oOo --

The Education Committee received a letter signed by members of the staff at Hawthorn at their June 1940 meeting, intimating that the staff were unanimous in the view that until ample shelter in the way of substantial dugouts was available the school should be closed altogether, but at least for those under seven.

The Head Teacher was interviewed by Committee and every step would be taken to speed up the completion of shelters.

-- oOo --

179

Miss Anstey resigns after 36 years service to local education on 31st October 1940.

-- oOo --

The Pavilion School opened September 1941 with 40 infants. The Grove School opened a little later the same year.

-- oOo --

Minutes of October 1943 indicated pressure on accommodation at Hawthorn. The Committee Secretary was instructed to communicate with the Board "Could a prefabricated hutment be added to the accommodation at the Pavilion School?"

The Board of Education refused the request so the Education Committee decided to make further representation in three months time.

-- oOo --

An inspection, repair and overhaul of children's respirators was to be carried out by the end of February 1944.

-- oOo --

During February 1944 Mr. Laundon was granted a cycle allowance of £1.10.0d per annum re journeys made as Caretaker of Hawthorn to The Grove and to the Pavilion School.

-- oOo --

Captain Hudson (Headmaster) to return July 1945! Mr. Moule had been the stand-by Head for 5½ years, whilst Captain Hudson served in World War II.

-- oOo --

The School Hymn

> We build our School on Thee, O Lord,
> To Thee we bring our common need,
> The loving heart, the gentle word,
> The tender thought, the kindly deed.

180

With these we pray, Thy spirit may
Enrich and bless our School alway.

We work together in Thy sight,
We live together in Thy love,
Guide Thou our faltering steps aright
And lift our thoughts to Heaven above.
Dear Lord we pray, Thy spirit may
Be present in our School alway.

Hold Thou each hand to keep it just,
Touch Thou our lips and make them pure.
If Thou art with us, Lord, we must
Be faithful friends and comrades sure.
Dear Lord we pray, Thy spirit may
Be present in our School alway.

We change, but Thou art still the same,
The same good Master, Teacher, Friend;
We change, but Lord we bear Thy name
To journey with it to the end.
And so we pray, Thy spirit may
Be present in our School alway.

This was the school hymn, which prevailed during Mr. Woods period as Headmaster. It seems that it was sung at certain prize giving ceremonies and according to Nick Andic (1956-1962) also at the end of term assembly.

-- oOo --

It was during the mid to late 1950's, following the demolition of the two large houses to the north of the school (Nos. 55 and 57 Broadway) which had originally been owned by Charles Pollard and which fronted onto Broadway, that the whole site was purchased for the school. Consequently, all of the land from Hawthorn Road right through to Broadway then belonged to the school. During July 1959, £600 was put aside for seeding the land and in 1980 the playground adjacent to Broadway was resurfaced. Entrance gates were erected and vehicular access was possible from Hawthorn Road through to Broadway.

History shows us several connections between the school and Charles Pollard:

181

1. The original plot in Hawthorn Road had been purchased from him in order that the school could be built during 1894-1895.
2. The school used London Road Hall (which he had had built during 1891) as an overflow classroom, during World War II.
3. Now the site, where his home was, in which he and his family had lived for many years, had been sold to the school and is now currently used as a playground.

-- oOo --

Eleven years old Caroline Gunn (daughter of Dr. and Mrs. A. Gunn) a pupil of Hawthorn had her poem entitled "The Stranger" read out on a BBC School Broadcast this morning. So reported the E.T. of 6th July 1964.

-- oOo --

The school from the 1960's was always a main player at the Kettering and District Schools Drama Festival and the Kettering Schools Music Festival. Rave notices were often received for performances which were latterly fine tuned by teachers Margaret Watson and Paul Aucott, to the delight of packed audiences at various local venues.

KETTERING AND DISTRICT SCHOOLS

SEVENTH

DRAMA FESTIVAL

19 - 20 - 21 MARCH 1962

TUESDAY

ST. ANDREW'S JUNIOR SCHOOL

Farmer Tumbledown's Pig

Cast

TOBIAS TUMBLEDOWN	Keith Roberts
ROSIE TUMBLEDOWN	Christine Blaxley
TILLY TUMBLEDOWN	Anne Stirmey
POLLY TUMBLEDOWN	Hilary Glandfield
SAMUEL SNEER	Kevin Long
SALLY SNEER	Cynthia Neal
TOMMY SNEER	David Blanchard
OLD WOMAN	Mary Gwylym
MAYOR	Benny Duffin
MAYOR'S LADY	Jennifer Tillin
TOWN CRIER	John Dinsdale
EBENEZER GREEN	Geoffrey Cooper

VILLAGERS, STALL KEEPERS' ETC.

Scene, The Village Street. The play is based on an item—"We Make a Play"—in a book by Maisie Cobby. It began as part of a Drama lesson and has been elaborated upon to include as many children as possible.

HAWTHORN ROAD SCHOOL

"The Play of the Weather" by G. MOUNTFORD WILLIAMS

Cast in order of appearance:

FROST	Vivien Cole
FOG	Stephen Fowtrell
RAIN	Elizabeth Tingle
LIGHTNING	Julie Howard
THUNDER	Malcolm Coe
SNOW	Carol Ash
HAIL	Peter Ford
ANNOUNCER	Robert Wells
WIND	Linda Wright
RAINBOW	Ailene Tether
CHAIRMAN OF UNIVERSAL WEATHER, LTD.	Susan Hegarty
1ST CLOUD	Elizabeth Dorr
2ND CLOUD	Gwyneth Clark
3RD CLOUD	Catherine Howard
SUN	Christine Lawrence
CRICKETER	Peter Hayward
UMBRELLA MAN	Janet Andrews
NEWS-REEL MAN	Brian Sharrocks
WASHERWOMAN	Pamela Adkins
1ST BOY	John Rootham
2ND BOY	Ian Lewis

The time is the present, the scene is "up in the clouds". The Weather Suppliers, after a quarrel amongst themselves, meet some of their Customers.

D.L. Photography

-- oOo --

182

Many former pupils will remember the "famous" merit system, which seemingly commenced whilst Mr. Woods was the Head. Stars were awarded for work and a certain number were required for a "merit". Some pupils may even remember that bad behaviour brought "demerits" with it!

All junior children belonged to a House (Montague, Buccleuch, Dalkeith or Gloucester) and each week the House with the most merits gained a coloured square on their chart which was displayed in the school hall. Competition was extremely keen, for at year end a trophy was awarded to the House with most merits.

-- oOo --

The E.T. of 9th October 1969 reported that David Dean was publishing a magazine for his fellow pupils. He was entitling it "The Weather" @ 2d per copy or 2/- annual subscription. He produced 13 copies as a first edition and sold out. When he produced his 11th and final copy during February 1970, sales had grown to 120, but in the meantime he had decided to change the title to "Science and News", as he wanted to widen the appeal of the magazine. Sadly, production had to end as he was soon to join the Grammar School and he wished to spend more time studying the stars, via a telescope he had bought for £4, and he was also saving for a chemistry set. He was hoping to join the meteorological and junior science societies whilst at Grammar School.

(With this background what can David Dean be doing now? – C.H.)

-- oOo --

The E.T. of 18th June 1970 reports that Jonathan Austin and Jeremy Sullivan of Hawthorn were both given books as their prizes in an annual contest, organized by the county branch of the "Men of the Trees" Society, which is designed to stimulate interest in the countryside.

-- oOo --

It was late 1970 when Alison Gunn, a ten year old was sitting with her friends at Hawthorn listening to a BBC programme entitled "Listening and Writing" she heard one of her own compositions

183

entitled "An Irritating Night" read out to school children all over the country.

Headteacher D.A. Woods explained that this was the second occasion that the school had been featured on the programme. He went on to reveal that the first occasion had been six years earlier and Alison's elder sister Caroline had been the contributor!!

-- o0o --

Anna Stean aged 11, used her imagination and skill to win a prize in a literary contest sponsored by the Daily Mirror, reported the E.T. of 24th March 1971. Anna entered the competition whilst in her last year at Hawthorn.

-- o0o --

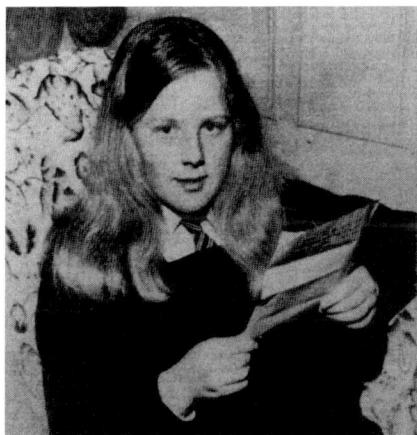

Kettering Evening Telegraph
Anna Stean

Kettering Evening Telegraph
Michael Smart and bicycle

Ten year old Michael Smart entered an E.T. road safety competition, colouring a picture and listing the errors in it. Much to his amazement he won the major prize of a Dawes bicycle. The County Road Safety Organiser told the E.T. that there was an extremely good response of a high standard, to the competition. (E.T. 23rd May 1972).

-- o0o --

184

An old playshed had been converted into a remedial teaching room by W.R. Burgess and Sons, on a plan drawn up by parent architect B. Austin. The P.T.A. footed the bill. September 1972.

-- oOo --

"Hawthorn is a thriving community and I hope that in addition to academic and sporting pursuits we give the children a good social training" – Peter Findlay, Headteacher, Autumn Term Report 1974.

-- oOo --

During its history, the school has produced some great chess players.

Taking a snapshot from the 1970's and 1980's we find that at the Kettering and District Primary School Chess Tournament of 1976, Hawthorn entered 15 children in the KO competition. At the quarter final stage all 8 contestants were from Hawthorn!! Eventually Andrew Draper ran out the winner over his schoolmates!

During 1977 five chess section members were selected for the Town Team and indeed the minutes of the School Governors meeting of 22 June gave great credit to Miss Brooks, the Team Coach for her dedication and enthusiasm that contributed to the success of the five and indeed to the success of the chess section.

The following two years (1978 and 1979) were also very good years for the school teams, in fact the overall team performances at November 1979 showed a playing record of P36 : W. 33 : D2 : L1. The "B" Team won its league without tasting defeat, whilst overall the school became County Champions for the second year running, beating the three other winners of the school leagues within Northamptonshire.

During Spring 1980 in the E.T. Individual Competition, which attracted 141 entrants, Hawthorn provided the winner in James Barr and the runner up in Hugh Ransley. James and Hugh followed up this success by also winning the Under 12 and Under 10 Championships respectively. The following year Hugh again excelled in becoming the 3rd Year County Champion and during April 1982 he showed great consistency becoming the Kettering

185

and District overall champion and also picking up the award as the Under 12 Champion in addition, to mark a tremendous run of success.

Further triumphs followed in the E.T. Championships, as in 1984, Jeremy Lines won his age group trophy, whilst during 1987 Andrew Bickle won the 4th Year Championship, defeating school mate William Branford in the final. However William won consolation by becoming the Under 12 Individual Champion.

The pupils continued playing chess until the early years of the 21st Century. However interest fell away, other attractions came to the fore and at the moment (June 2007), chess is not an option for the pupils. Possibly when a new teacher arrives who is a keen chess player, matters may change once more!

-- oOo --

D.L. Photography

The apple tree that stands in the playground, on the part that was purchased during the 1950's, subsequently was blessed with an encircling wooden seat, which was constructed under the care of the then Deputy Head, Mike Coleman. During summer months classes are still taken outside so that the children are able to listen to stories from underneath the spreading branches. It is often said that the stories are made so much more interesting by being told in these particularly pleasant circumstances.

-- oOo --

186

Mike Coleman tells of the school not having a flagpole. This fact used to irritate him on certain days when it would have been appropriate to have "flown the flag". He decided to act therefore and use the connections that he had in his home town of Corby to fulfill his plan. He persuaded a close friend, Derek Wathey, to donate a Union Jack, Corby Grampian Club kindly came up with a Scottish Saltire and Mike himself donated the flag of St. George to the school. Clive Chenery the Plant Manger of the British Steel Lamp Standard Dept. at Corby supervised the manufacture and delivery of a large flagpole and base which was kindly delivered to Hawthorn by lorry. Then Bernie Burt, a local contractor who did work for the School on occasions, made a suitable hole and sank the base in concrete. So at last a flagpole was born.

Thereafter on all appropriate occasions the flags were run up the flagpole. Indeed there was even rumour of the Jolly Roger being flown on certain days, Mike of course being a most responsible Deputy Head, at that time, hotly denies this!

-- oOo --

During the mid 1980's a "practical area" had been developed within the playground, which included a small nature pool. By October 1987 it had become very well established and to great excitement it had been visited by a frog!!

A Nene College scientist had also visited and had concluded that the ecology was excellent!

-- oOo --

Mrs. Margaret Watson retired Christmas 1987 following 17 years at Hawthorn. Many children will remember her fantastic contribution to music over the years (Head Teacher report February 1988).

-- oOo --

Six eleven year old girls known as the Dipping Dolphins, had been working on five challenges since February (Evening Telegraph 24th June 1998). They had been making 3D models of endangered species in a campaign of awareness. Their efforts were sponsored by AWA who were so impressed with the efforts of the girls that a

187

cheque for £300 was presented to the school in recognition of their excellence.

-- oOo --

Damage to the ceiling of the school hall has resulted in the whole hall area being cordoned off to ensure the safety of the children and staff of the school. We are in the process of arranging for a full structural survey to be completed, which will reveal the full extent of the damage.

Until the results of this have been obtained we need to ensure that everyone at Hawthorn remains safe. In the short term we have relocated certain classes away from the hall area, but in the longer term it may be necessary to find alternative solutions.

Scaffolding is currently being erected, which we hope will allow us to gain access to classes 2 and 6 which are currently out of action. However, until we are certain that the children's safety can be guaranteed we must make other arrangements.

We have only been able to accommodate the children from the affected classes this week because one class is absent from school on a residential visit. Once these children return to school on Monday 14th May 2007 there will not be enough teaching space for all classes.

As a result of this a rota has been devised which will require one class per day to remain at home. Your child should bring home a letter on Thursday which gives further details of which classes are affected.

We will of course keep all parents updated on the situation as soon as further information becomes available.

During May 2007 this news appeared on the school website. "Following professional inspection, the damage was not thought to be quite as bad as first expected, but the scaffolding had to remain and the classrooms were to be kept out of use until further notice. The start of the Autumn Term however had to be put back one week in order to accommodate the restoration work and the cleaning."

188

No doubt it would be small comfort to staff and pupils to be aware that this was not the first occasion that Hawthorn had experienced ceiling problems. The School Management and General Purposes Sub-committee minutes of Monday 6th June 1904 report that the ceiling of the west classroom of Hawthorn Road School (front of building, Garfield Street side) was in such condition as to be dangerous. Mr. O.P. Drever to attend to it forthwith.

-- oOo --

Throughout my research for this book, time and time again, I found the subject of "school toilets" was highlighted. The toilets were blocked, needed repair, too far away, needed decorating, smelly and so on and so forth. For many years the school toilets were never as staff, parents, pupils and governors would have wished: When requests for improvement were made, "lack of money", "low priority" were the usual negative responses.

Eventually new toilets were provided and appear perfectly adequate at the moment. Let us therefore now hope that forevermore the Hawthorn toilets are perfectly functioning, perfectly decorated and exotically perfumed!!

-- oOo --

Kettering Evening Telegraph

Champion Soccer Team April 1972

189

Music class in the hall with Judy Barney and Linda Dix

What's going on here? With teacher Karen Barkley

190

Miss Morris with her sleepy heads

A typical 2008 classroom scene

191

Miss Barr's class prefer the floor

Miss Hedley keeps attention

School hall 1911. Coronation day of King George the Fifth, 22nd June. The flag from Tasmania is the backdrop

School hall 2000. The Millenium scene
The flag from Tasmania is again the backdrop.

Mrs. Curtis, Support Assistant in a one-to-one session.

Miss Barber gets 'arty'

195

Mrs. Shackleton settles in a corner of the Community Room

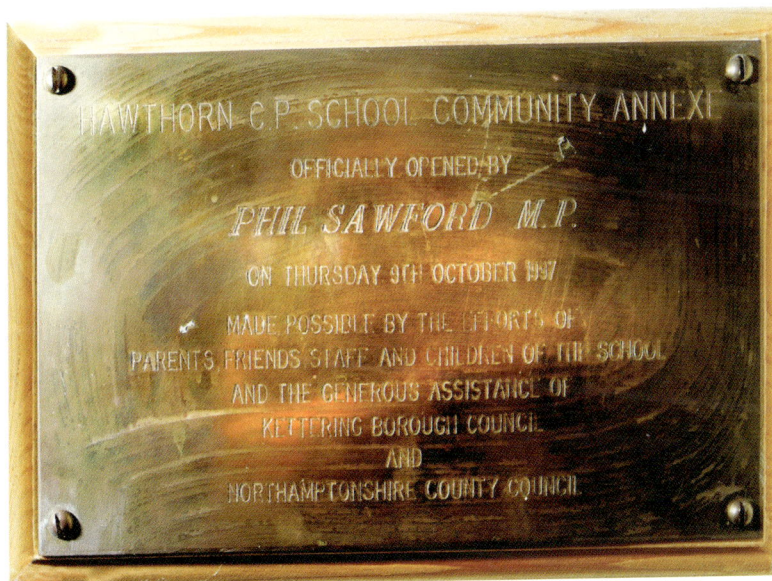

The plaque showing the opening of the School extension on 9 October 1997 by
Phil Sawford, Member of Parliament for Kettering

196

Miss Tyrell watches over a busy play area

Miss Park spells it out

197

Hawthorn Head Teachers

Infants Department

1 May 1895 – 31 May 1907	Miss Elizabeth Ann Clarke
June 1907 – 6 November 1911	Miss G.A. Clapp

-- oOo --

Mixed Department

30 October 1905 – November 1916	William H. Cartwright
December 1916 – 18 February 1917	J.G. Gidney
March 1917 – 1919	J.W. Smith
1919 – 28 April 1931	Edgar Markham
May 1931 – May 1939	Captain William Hudson
May 1939 – June 1945	A.F. Moule – Acting Head whilst Captain Hudson served in World War II
July 1945 – 1946	Captain William Hudson
1947 – 1952	L. Bird
1952 – 1973	D.A. Woods
1974 – 1984	P.A. Findlay
1984 –	Richard Hall

On 6 November 1911, the Board of Education agreed to the proposed amalgamation of the Infants and Mixed Departments of Hawthorn Road School, under William H. Cartwright the Head Teacher of the Mixed School.

-- oOo --

Some Caretakers / Site Supervisors that we knew and loved at Hawthorn

Mrs. Z. Cooper	From 22 April 1895 to 13 January 1908
Mr. C.S. Cooper (son of Mrs. Z. Cooper)	13 January 1908 to 12 January 1925
Miss Wallis*	November 1917 to November 1919
Mr. A. Price*	
Mrs. Wills*	

(*The three above named served as temporary caretakers whilst Mr. Cooper served his country during World War I)

Mr. E.C. Laundon	1928 to 1959
Mr. Clarke	1959 to 1963
Mrs. Beasley	1963 to 1965
Mr. L. Buckby	1969 to 11 March 1980
Mr. J.R. Morrows	1 April 1980 to 31 March 1988
Mr. Catling	14 March 1988 to 6 April 1990
David Hurcombe†	11 June 1990 to 10 January 1998
Stuart Moore†	1 February 1998 to July 2006
Bob Althorpe†	July 2006 to November 2006
Stuart Holt†	October 2006 to present

† Site Supervisor from June 1990

-- oOo --

Maureen Buckerfield Collection

Mrs. Taylor's class of 1954.

Finally, in conclusion, I make no apology in recalling the words of Mamie Hooper and trust that future Hawthorn generations take note and act upon these sentiments!

"Work hard boys and girls of Hawthorn Road, value your school, and above all, value the friendships you will make, and may they last a lifetime!"

-- oOo --

School Orchestra 1978

SELF CONFIDENCE – INDEPENDENCE – MOTIVATION

-- oOo --   *-- oOo --*   *-- oOo --*

-

BIBLIOGRAPHY

Aldwinkle School Days – Janet Sharman 2005

Kettering Town Cricket League – A Personal View – Dave Short 2005

The Development and Structure of the English School System – Keith Evans 1985

Kelly's Directories (various)

Tony Iresons series of books "Old Kettering A View from the 1930's"

Kettering School Board Minutes 1895-1902

Kettering Urban District Council Education Committee School Management and General Purposes Sub-Committee Minutes 1901-1944

Certain School records were utilised as follows:

Punishment Book	13 October 1931 – 2 September 1981
Call Book	16 July 1936 – June 1947
Scrapbooks	September 1959 – April 1973
Log Book	10 April 1972 – 20 July 1990
School Managers Minutes	8 February 1974 – 8 February 2004

-- oOo --   -- oOo --   -- oOo --